Be a Wiccan Badass
Become More Confident and Unleash Your Inner Power

from GoddessHasYourBack.com

Moonwater SilverClaw
Wiccan High Priestess
Blogger/Founder of
GoddessHasYourBack.com
with visitors from **173 countries**

A QuickBreakthrough Publishing Edition

Copyright © 2017 Johanna Ellen Mac Leod
ISBN: 0998427306
ISBN-13: 978-0998427300

All rights reserved. No part of this book may be reproduced or transmitted in any form by any means electronic or mechanical, including photocopying, recording or by any information storage and retrieval system without written permission from the publisher.

More copies are available from the publisher with the imprint QuickBreakthrough Publishing. For more information about this book contact: askawitchnow@gmail.com

This book was developed and written with care. Names and details were modified to respect privacy.

Disclaimer: The author and publisher acknowledge that each person's situation is unique, and that readers have full responsibility to seek consultations with health, financial, spiritual and legal professionals. The author and publisher make no representations or warranties of any kind, and the author and publisher shall not be liable for any special, consequential or exemplary damages resulting, in whole or in part, from the reader's use of, or reliance upon, this material.:

Other Books by Moonwater SilverClaw:
- Goddess Has Your Back
- Goddess Walks Beside You
- The Hidden Children of the Goddess
- Beyond the Law of Attraction to Real Magick
- Goddess Reveals Your Enchanted Light

Praise for Moonwater SilverClaw:

• "In her book *The Hidden Children of the Goddess*, Moonwater brings Wicca to life, enveloping you in the mystery and magick of the Craft. Her writing talent is amazing! Her kindness and even sense of fun is ever present throughout her writing. Moonwater expresses profound Wicca concepts through examples in her own life experience. Wicca actually saved her life. and empowered her to leave an abusive marriage, and this shows the power of this sacred path to positively change the course of our lives, too. Moonwater's stories personally inspire me, and I am confident that they will inspire you also." – Rev. Patrick McCollum, internationally recognized spiritual leader working for human rights, social justice, and equality; the 2010 recipient of the Mahatma Gandhi Award for the Advancement of Pluralism.

• "Religion scholars in the future will likely view Moonwater SilverClaw as the pivotal voice that helped change the discourse on Wicca. In her book **Goddess Has Your Back,** Moonwater reveals Wicca as a very positive and ultimately uplifting spirituality choice. She demystifies the religion's taboos and spooky stereotypes through her unintimidating presentation that clarifies the topic. She introduces the Goddess and the magick rituals that, when used properly, can positively impact your everyday life. The author relays her very personal perspective on the subject and shows how to integrate the philosophies and practices of the centuries-old religion. Looking for a fresh perspective on spiritual growth? Read what Moonwater SilverClaw has to say. She may very well point you in the direction where you need to go." – Stacy D. Horn

• "Moonwater's writing will give you a portrait of a woman who lives her faith, and whose life was saved by it. Because so many lives, my own included, were irrevocably changed by Wicca, were given new focus, new purpose, and perhaps most importantly, new personal power to realize one's dreams and ambitions. . . . It's a story about making your own happy endings, about rescuing yourself, and that, I believe, is what makes writing like this necessary." – Jason Pitzl-Waters, blogger at WildHunt.org

Visit Moonwater's blog: www.GoddessHasYourBack.com

Moonwater SilverClaw

CONTENTS*

These are highlights. There is much more material in this book!

Dedication and Acknowledgments	6
Be a Wiccan Badass	7
Section One: Connect with God and Goddess	8
Section Two: Be Smart and Knowledgeable	21
Section Three: Have Energy	45
A Spell to Attract New and Positive Friends	55
Section Four: Make Things Happen	79
Should I Create Spells or Follow a Book?	83
How to Do an Effective Money Spell	97
Section Five: Protect Yourself	109
The Wiccan Badass Protects Herself from Toxic People	133
Section Six: Know You're Here to Serve	143
About the Author; Special Offer to Reader of this Book	161
Excerpt from *Goddess Has Your Back*	163
Excerpt from *Beyond the Law of Attraction to Real Magick*	169

DEDICATION AND ACKNOWLEDGEMENTS

This book is dedicated to the God and Goddess. Thanks to Tom Marcoux for editing. Thanks to Kay Pannell for her guidance and friendship.

Be A Wiccan Badass

When have you wanted to act like a badass?

At nineteen, I really could have used a crash course in being a badass. Why? At the time, I was scrambling to stay alive in an abusive marriage.

I needed to experience a shift in myself. Fortunately, my path in Wicca helped me become stronger. Instead of remaining trapped with my then-husband, *I left*. Wicca also strengthened me to become bold. I had to shake off my fear due to enduring dyslexia as a kid. It took courage to become a blogger/author.

In this book, we discuss how *you* can become a Wiccan Badass. *You can be more confident when you solidify a connection with the Goddess.* Even if someone insults you, you can carry yourself with grace and strength because you know the Gods are with you.

I've noticed that in popular culture "badass" seems to have two major definitions:

- "of formidable strength or skill" (merriam-webster.com)
- "distinctively tough or powerful; so exceptional as to be intimidating" (dictionary.com)

Badass, at least in some movies, appears to mean someone "who does not care and who will do anything." We often see a badass character in a movie doing something outrageous.

My definition of badass is about "being confident and strong."

To me, a badass is someone who makes her own choices. Someone who has more great moments in life because she takes action. This person has more capacity to handle tough things that arise in life.

A Wiccan Badass is something extra. She's a person who's tuned into the power and love from God and Goddess. Sure, she has more moments of *feeling confident.* Why? Because she has extra and important knowledge. And she has gained special experiences that deepen her connection with God and Goddess. *A Wiccan Badass stands up for herself.* A Wiccan Badass is wise. She knows when to use her strength and when not to.

Through this book, you can make a shift so you enjoy more confident moments.

Are you ready to learn the ways of a Wiccan Badass?

I thought so!

First, here are Six Actions of being a Wiccan Badass:
1. Connect with God and Goddess.
2. Be smart and knowledgeable.
3. Have energy.
4. Make things happen.
5. Protect yourself.
6. Know you're here to serve.

Do I always act as a Wiccan Badass? No. I'm learning and growing. I make mistakes. Still, I can say this: *I'm much stronger than ever before.* I've learned from my elders in the

Wiccan community. And I've walked my own path of discovery and empowerment. And yes, Wicca helped me to strengthen myself to leave that abusive marriage. **Being strong and doing what's necessary is badass.**

Let's get started.

SECTION ONE
Connect with God and Goddess

"You're so damn stupid. What were you thinking? I told you be home at 6 pm!" my then-husband yelled at me. Instead of letting his rage hit me, I blocked this disempowering energy through the use of *shielding*. **God and Goddess had helped me to know** that I was *not* trash. So, I practiced the process of shielding which I'll share below.

My definition of a Wiccan Badass is: Someone who does these three things:
- Seizes choices
- Gains knowledge
- Acts decisively

In this case, I began with gaining knowledge from the God and Goddess through meditation.

Fortunately, I had completed a meditation session before my then-husband had returned home for the second time that evening. The first time, he had returned to an empty house and that had pissed him off.

During my meditation session, I had fortified my shield.

How to Do Shielding:
Go to someplace safe. You could even do your brief

shielding process in a bathroom stall. Breathe in and out—and feel your feet on the ground. Reach down with your consciousness and take a deep breath. Visualize pulling up the energy of Mother Earth through your feet and up your body.

Continue to pull the energy into your chest, then up to the top of your head. Then with your arms, push the energy out into a sphere around you. Envision a white, greenish light surrounding you. Concentrate for a moment to make sure the sphere of light is stable. Know that no bad energies can reach you with your shield up. Feel the strength of the shield. *You are now shielded.*

My practice of shielding strengthened me so much that I became strong enough to divorce my then-husband.

To me, divorcing my husband was a Wiccan Badass action.

My then-husband had failed to treat me respectfully as part of the Goddess.

The structure of this book is that I communicate a story about one of the six elements of being a Wiccan Badass, and I follow that with separate methods.

For example, we'll now continue with ...

Connect with God and Goddess #1

In Just One Moment, Connect with Goddess

"I was so happy a day ago," my friend Anna said.

"I hear a 'but' coming up," I said.

"But then I found out my project is going to cost three times more," she said.

"That sounds tough to hear," I replied. "What were you happy about?"

"Our project had a new donor," she continued, "But now, we're stuck."

I empathize with Anna's situation.

The strange thing I notice is that Anna did not immediately invoke her Wiccan knowledge. Why did that happen?

You see, your ordinary, daily life is NOT separate from your spiritual life.

What could Anna do—in just a moment or two—to help her feel the Goddess's love?

Turn Your Thoughts to Goddess

Shift to your feelings and thoughts about what you're grateful for. Use this chant:

Gracious Lady of the Moon,
I thank you now for this boon.

Light a Candle per day

You can light a candle as an offering to express your gratitude for what you do have.

On the first day, Anna could have lit a candle to express her gratitude for the project donation.

On the second day, Anna could light a candle for Goddess's Guidance.

Use this chant:

Goddess,
I don't know what to do.

Grant me strength to find a solution.
Guide me with Your Divine Inspiration.

Grant me strength to find a solution.
Guide me with Your Divine Inspiration.

Grant me strength to find a solution.
Guide me with Your Divine Inspiration.

So Mote It Be.

The third day would be time to do an offering after what you want has manifested.

Find some humor.
When we do things, we'll face some resistance.
I was talking with a friend recently and we came up with this little phrase:

Goddess,
I thank you now.
I thank you later.
Do what You will
to straighten out this hater.

My friend and I laughed about this one.
Remember, you can connect with Goddess in just one moment.

Section One
Connect with God and Goddess #2

Five Ways to Connect with God and Goddess

"You say that it's important to connect with God and Goddess. But I just don't understand. It feels like a really big thing," Andrea said.

In answer, I shared with her the following five methods for drawing closer to God and Goddess.

1) Prayer to the Moon
You could talk to the moon. I once mentioned this a friend, Shirley. Her face crinkled in confusion. I explained that I look upon the moon as a representation of the Goddess. Sure, I know that the moon is a celestial body that effects the tides.

And still, when I look up, I experience the moon as a beautiful representation of the Goddess.

When on a walk with my sweetheart, I often exclaim,

"Oh! Look at the moon. Isn't she beautiful!"
Here is a prayer you can express to the Moon:

My sweet gracious Lady of the Moon.
Shine Your light upon me now,
May you hear my call to know You.
Here me O-Lovely Lady
I, (your name here), am here to adore You.
I am here to listen to Your song in the night,
Your whispers upon the breeze.
Here my call to You O-Great Mother.
May You answer my prayers.
So mote it be.

I often can feel it in my heart that Goddess *is* listening. She *is* there.

2) Prayer at Dawn to the God

Greeting the sun as it rises is a great way to meet the God. Here is a prayer you can express to the God:

Blessings to thee O-Great and powerful Lord of the Sun.
I greet You this fine morning.
You have blessed me.
Shine upon me with Your blessed light.
Hear me O-Lord, my need for Your love and connection.
I, (your name here), call upon Your wisdom.
Share with me your thoughts.
Speak to me O-Great Lord.
May You answer my prayers.
So mote it be.

3) A Walk in Nature

To connect with God and Goddess, it's important to separate yourself from your routine thoughts and cares. Use this prayer as a way to immerse yourself in the present moment. Soak in, through your senses, the scent of the fresh air, the caress of the breeze on your face, and the delightful view of flowers and trees.

Express this prayer:

May I be in this present moment and know You.
God and Goddess, You are here with me,
As I walk my sacred path.
Here I feel the ground beneath my feet,
Treading the sacred path.
And as I breathe in the air of life, I know You.
As I walk under this, Your beautiful sky, I see You.
As the air caresses my skin this present moment, I feel You.
Surrounded by your creations, the birds, the trees and the Sky,
I am here in Your Temple, the Earth.
You are here and now.
Blessed be my path.
So mote it be.

4) Light a Candle

It seemed like a miracle: I easily found a parking space in San Francisco! (Yes, they do exist.) I immediately resolved to light a candle in honor of the Parking Goddess as soon as I returned home.

In general, lighting a candle and saying a prayer is an easy and brief way for you to connect with the God and Goddess.

Use simple phrases. Perhaps, something like:

Lord and Lady, I light this candle
As an offering in thanks for _____.
May You find it pleasing.
So mote it be.

Warning: Do NOT leave a burning candle unattended. Make sure the candle burns all the way down.

5) Meditate

Try to create a daily meditation practice. My sweetheart devotes three minutes every morning before he turns on any electronic device. He tells me that even if he feels that urgent email is waiting for him, he can spare three minutes.

With a regular meditation practice, you can build a relationship with the God and Goddess. I find that my meditation practice has given me opportunities to hear insights from the God and Goddess.

May you find one or more of these five practices to enrich your Wiccan Badass path.

Section One
Connect with God and Goddess #3

Call Upon the Goddess and God

The Goddess gently held my left hand, and I could feel Her loving energy flow into my hand. Then the God took my right hand in His.

I felt so comforted, and this is when I knew in the core of my being that Wicca and my connection with God and Goddess were absolutely real.

Today, I was surprised. A dear friend asked me how often do I recall this experience that arose in one of my meditation sessions.

"Not often," I replied.

"You don't purposely reconnect with those feelings and that memory each week?" my friend asked.

"No, I don't. Usually I find life to be too busy," I said.

Wait a minute! Is this how I want my life to be?

What would I like my life to be? Less chaotic!

Now, let's pause for a moment. **To be a Wiccan Badass,**

you need to be strong. There is a certain form of strength that rises from a calm and peaceful core.

It seems that many of us are searching for that.

My friend asked, "When, during your week, is your life less chaotic?"

Recently, I've made more efforts to meditate in the morning.

I've experienced peace and even a sense of accomplishment.

That's a foundation to build our Wiccan Badass approach to life.

Now, pause for a minute. When you could you set aside even just five minutes for meditation?

Could you take a 10-minute walk during your lunch hour?

Could you start a window sill garden to include something growing in your life?

God and Goddess are present in the everyday world. Still, we need to slow down and make space so we can become aware of Their Presence.

When you're driving and you come to a stoplight, you could take in a deep breath, see the blue sky, and say, "Thank you God and Goddess for this lovely blue sky." That would be something simple to remind yourself that God and Goddess are near you.

Section One
Connect with God and Goddess #4

What is the Wiccan View of "Perfect Love and Perfect Trust"?

"I just don't understand it," my friend, John, said.
"Understand what?" I asked.
"When am I going to start to feel better? When will I start to feel safe? When will I feel this Perfect Love and Perfect Trust?" he asked.

I could relate to his situation. It was not until I was 18 years old, that I had an experience of perfect love and trust. How? It was during a meditation session. That's when I felt two Presences beside me. The God was on my left, and the Goddess was on my right. They each took one of my hands. Words pale in trying to express the energy I felt. The experience was a transfer of love, compassion, and peace. I felt safe, and finally I felt like I belonged.

If only I could just give this experience to John.

Frequently, I describe Wicca as an experiential, spiritual path. This is not just about studying sacred texts. *No*. It is in meditation and ritual ... it is in walking through this world that we have an *experience* that fully informs us that God and Goddess are present.

I describe the experience of "perfect love and perfect trust" with this metaphor: A blind person sits in a room. She's distracted as she runs her hand quickly over braille in her book. She is unaware that the God and Goddess are present in the room. Still, the God and Goddess wait until she reaches her hands out—and then, lovingly, God and Goddess take her hands. They guide her safely from the room. She needs to fully love and trust the God and Goddess and that they will guide her well.

We turn toward the God and Goddess. If you don't watch for the signs from the God and Goddess, and if you don't trust in Their guidance, you'll miss out.

Sometimes, things go awry. We wonder why bad things seem to be happening to us. However, we need to trust the Gods and realize that they have a bigger plan to help us learn and grow. What is most important now? Learn to connect with the God and Goddess.

I would recommend that you take even small steps toward the God and Goddess. Consider even just a daily five-minute meditation session. Perform a simple candle-lighting ritual.

Begin.

Section Two
Be Smart and Knowledgeable

My mentor said, "You forgot one vital detail."

"Yes?" I asked, my eyes bright with my eagerness to do one of my first spells correctly.

"You need to include this phrase, 'May it harm none,'" she said.

"Oh," I said. "What would happen if I failed to include that?"

"God and Goddess have a larger perspective than us. What could happen is that you get what you want in this moment, but it ultimately hurts you or someone else later. God and Goddess see the whole picture and know what can go wrong. And they know what is best for you," my mentor emphasized.

As I mentioned earlier, my definition of a Wiccan Badass is someone who does these three things:

- Seizes choices
- Gains knowledge
- Acts decisively

This section is about the vital information you need so that when you act, you're acting in effective ways. At this point, I'll share what I find to be the distinction between "be smart" and "be knowledgeable."

- To be smart is to acting intelligently.
- To be knowledgeable is to have a storehouse of information in your brain.

The Wiccan Badass has both. She acts intelligently while using excellent information.

On the other hand, someone else might be knowledgeable but fail to act appropriately. How often have you heard a friend say, "I know I should do that, but somehow, I just fail to get around to it"? That's tragic.

Instead, use the following information so you act as an effective Wiccan Badass.

Section Two
Be Smart and Knowledgeable #1

What Are the Signs of a Natural Born Witch?

As I reflected on my own journey, I realized that it was the combination of the below characteristics that revealed my hidden nature as a witch. I do note that one can view a separate characteristic as a sign that one may be an empath or clairvoyant or something else.

1) You make offerings to nature

When I was about five years old, I could feel the Goddess. I just didn't know Who She was. I just felt it was the Spirit of

Nature that I was sensing. I felt good in nature, so I gave it offerings. I would collect berries and set them up in a nice place for this Spirit of Nature.

2) You know things before they happen

When I was seven, I stepped into the kitchen. My father and brother were trying to fix some camping equipment. I knew something was going to happen. I just KNEW it. So, I ran from the kitchen and into the patio. I paced, scared as a rabbit in its den, threatened by a fox at its doorway.

BOOOOMMMMM! The sound burst from the kitchen. I ran back to that room to see my brother being rushed from the floor to the shower. He had been burned. A lantern had exploded, burning the ceiling and both my dad and my brother. We ended up at the hospital.

3) You find peace and sacredness in nature

Whenever I was in the natural world outside, I could feel the Spirit of Nature and a deep resounding peace. This was different from the God of the Christians I heard about on Sunday at church. There was nothing harsh, judgmental, or angry about the Spirit of Nature. Her energy was peaceful and kind. Whenever I was outside with the plants, trees, and animals, I felt safe. I belonged.

4) You have a gift

In my late teens, I realized that I had an ability to pick up the energy of other people in a deep way. Sometimes, this felt like a gift because I could relate well and warm up my relationships. Other times, this felt like a burden because negative emotions would beat me up inside.

* * *

Again, I'm talking about having some form of combination related to the above characteristics.

If you find yourself in the above descriptions, you just may be a natural born witch.

Section Two
Be Smart and Knowledgeable #2

Is Magic Real? Is the Universe Magic? Is Everything Magic?

"Is magic real? Is the universe magic? Is everything magic?" asked one of my readers.

In response, my first thought was: "Yes, magick is real. Magick, at its basic form, is energy. Energy permeates the universe. So yes, the universe is magick. Everything is made of energy so again, yes—everything is magick."

Recently, I was interviewed on The Buzz, a show on ztalkradio.com, and I went deeper with the idea of magick as energy.

First, I mentioned the energy that is inside a bolt of lightning.

When the bolt strikes a tree, it changes the tree. Therefore, energy and magick have physical capabilities and properties.

At this point, we can reference science. The molecules of

H20 (water) change form depending how fast they are moving. When they move slowly, we have ice. A bit faster, and we have water. Moving quite quickly—and the water becomes a gas. It's all about energy.

As I mentioned, everything is made of energy.

"We are all connected to each other biologically, to the earth chemically and to the rest of the universe atomically. That's kinda cool! That makes me smile and I actually feel quite large at the end of that. It's not that we are better than the universe, we are part of the universe. We are in the universe and the universe is in us."
– Neil deGrasse Tyson, physicist

Wiccans take a big responsibility when they wield magick.

Section Two
Be Smart and Knowledgeable #3

Discover Your Wiccan Destiny

"I don't understand. Some spiritual paths say that we choose what we're going to learn in this current incarnation. I didn't ask to get attacked as a child," my friend Erica said.

"I hear you. I know that has caused you a lot of pain over the years," I said.

"I still want to know," she continued.

"I've come to know, for myself, that I chose the lessons for my life. But then the Universe took over to fulfill my order," I said.

"So, when I was between lifetimes, I decided what I wanted to learn? Did I want to learn how to endure? To become stronger? To have empathy for people who've gone through child abuse?" Erica asked.

"It could be. Only you would come to know the meaning of your own journey," I replied.

We, Wiccans, have an advantage. We know that the Gods

and the Goddesses want what is best for us. They do not "protect" us from the lessons we must learn.

A friend of mine said it this way: "We choose the lessons, but the Universe chooses the how."

I've come to realize that one's Wiccan Destiny is a combination of our choosing lessons and the Universe offering the stairs that we walk.

You might find this chant helpful:

Goddess,
Help me endure as I learn what I must
In you I trust.

Section Two
Be Smart and Knowledgeable #4

When to Share about Your Wiccan Path …

"You really have courage, Moonwater," Steven, one of my friends, said.

"How?"

"You talk openly about your Wiccan path," he said.

I've had a number of conversations with Wiccans who talk openly about their path and with others who do not and remain in the "broom closet."

When I attend work-networking events with one of my family members, I wear my pentacle (I always wear it) with a blouse that obscures it. Why? In his work, my family member encounters many different Christians from different sects. My thought is: if someone asks me I'll talk about my Wiccan path, but I will not "push" the attendees by displaying something that is personal to me.

My mentors emphasize that Wiccans do *not* proselytize. At Merriam-Webster.com, the definition of *proselytize* includes "to induce someone to convert to one's faith; to recruit someone to join one's party, institution, or cause."

On occasion, I have found an individual or two to be oppressive (or at least annoying) when someone was trying to convert me or recruit me for their religion.

When talking with Wiccan friends, I enjoy that we leave space for people to have their own individual practices and thoughts.

Wiccans get to choose what thoughts and beliefs we have, and we are not forced into someone else's beliefs like certain religions.

Section Two
Be Smart and Knowledgeable #5

Why the Misuse of "Warlock" is an Important Topic

"Why is the misuse of the term 'warlock' bothering you so much, Moonwater?" a dear friend asked me.

"Warlock is not the name for a male witch. A male witch is simply called a witch," I began.

Warlock is a derogatory term that means oath breaker and liar. Why is this important? In Wicca, oaths are an essential part of our whole spiritual path.

For example, as a 3rd Degree Wiccan Priestess, I am oath-bound to never reveal certain secret knowledge passed to me by my mentors. I do NOT share certain details with family members or friends who have NOT been initiated.

Wicca is a power path, and people can misuse such power. If a Wiccan breaks certain oaths, bad consequences will result. This is serious!

Furthermore, my journey of rising to 3rd degree occurred

over eight years. During that time, my mentor made sure that I was ready for deep and secret knowledge revealed at each level. This was about personal safety.

So, beware of the distortions that the media and other sources express.

Words have power, and they need to be used in the correct manner.

Section Two
Be Smart and Knowledgeable #6

Is It Possible to Practice Christian witchcraft?

One of my readers asked, "How can I begin practicing Christian witchcraft?"

Among many viewpoints, here are two in particular.

Viewpoint #1: Some people say they follow the example of Jesus, the Christ—and they want to learn how to use magick.

Viewpoint #2: Some Christians hold to a strict focus on certain quotes from the Bible. Some examples are:

Leviticus 20:27
"A man or a woman who is a medium or a necromancer shall surely be put to death. They shall be stoned with stones; their blood shall be upon them."

Deuteronomy 18:14
For these nations, which you are about to dispossess, listen to

fortune-tellers and to diviners. But as for you, the Lord your God has not allowed you to do this.
Micah 5:12
And I will cut off sorceries from your hand, and you shall have no more tellers of fortunes.

For those who believe that one must follow the Bible literally; these literalists would say that one cannot be both Christian and practice magick.

I have a concern about the words "Christian witchcraft." According to my own mentors, this phrase "Christian witchcraft" does NOT work. A witch is someone who honors the old Gods and Goddesses. That appears as a separation point. A Christian is called a "follower of Christ" and Jesus said that He is the Son of God [one is told not to honor any other God or Goddess.]

Could someone believe in Jesus and practice magick? It may be possible. But that person is not a witch. Maybe that person says that he or she is eclectic.

Note: Someone using magick without religion could be called a sorcerer. A Christian sorcerer would ***not*** be a witch.

Section Two
Be Smart and Knowledgeable #7

Why Is Sexism More Acceptable Than Racism?

I was sexually attacked when I was a teen. I share this fact considering recent events [This was noted at my blog GoddessHasYourBack.com] …

Brock Allen Turner, the former Stanford University student, was recently convicted of raping a 23-year-old woman (outside a Stanford frat party taking place on January 17, 2015). Turner attacked his victim while she was unconscious. Additionally, he took a photo of her breasts and shared this damn photo with his swim team buddies. For the criminal act of rape, he will only serve in jail for 3 months.

At least he can leave his cell one day. His victim is trapped forever in hers. I know something about this. As I mentioned, I was sexually attacked when I was a teen. I still can't leave the prison of my mind. The attack affected me then, and the attack still affects me now.

I have grown with therapy. Yes, I am a survivor. But no matter what window dressings you put on a cell, it's still a cell.

Turner's father said that his son should not have to go to prison for "20 minutes of action." This is not about 20 minutes. A person can lose a limb or be rendered paralyzed in the fraction of a second. We're not talking about time. We're talking about damage.

In this section, I'm talking about "Why is Sexism More Acceptable Than Racism?"

In a written statement, the 23-year-old woman-victim of Turner's CRIME, wrote: "He is a lifetime sex registrant. That doesn't expire. Just like what he did to me doesn't expire, doesn't just go away after a set number of years. It stays with me, it's part of my identity, it has forever changed the way I carry myself, the way I live the rest of my life. [You could use Google to find her complete statement.]

51.9% of American women experience physical violence in their lifetime.

What if 51.9% of white men had their arm cut off—do you think some preventative action would happen?

Maybe that is part of the problem here. Rape and its after effects are not something you can readily see.

Let's look at this further. Many men in countries around the world use women like tissue paper and then discard them like trash. In some countries women are considered property. In America, women are paid only 79 cents of each a dollar a man earns for the same work. Tell me that is not sexism.

In many places, a number of religions or sects of religion have supported sexism. Why are they pushing this archaic idea that women need to be obedient to men?

Imagine a better world in which equals, regardless of gender, are kind and supportive of one another. Certainly, Wicca honors the sacred feminine and honors equality.

The 23-year-old woman-victim of Turner's CRIME, ended her written statement with:

"And finally, to girls everywhere, I am with you. On nights when you feel alone, I am with you. When people doubt you or dismiss you, I am with you. I fought every day for you. So never stop fighting, I believe you. As the author Anne Lamott once wrote, "Lighthouses don't go running all over an island looking for boats to save; they just stand there shining." Although I can't save every boat, I hope that by speaking today, you absorbed a small amount of light, a small knowing that you can't be silenced, a small satisfaction that justice was served, a small assurance that we are getting somewhere, and a big, big knowing that you are important, unquestionably, you are untouchable, you are beautiful, you are to be valued, respected, undeniably, every minute of every day, you are powerful and nobody can take that away from you. To girls everywhere, I am with you."

When is the U.S. culture going to believe women, support women, and throw out archaic, horrible behavior toward women?

In American entertainment, women are beaten, raped and killed a lot.

However, American entertainment has progressed to have African-American characters in co-lead roles. Some African-American actors have their own television shows, feature films and more. (Hispanics and Asians are not always included.)

Apparently, showing non-racist depictions of ethnic characters has become a priority of some entertainment creators. So, racism, at least in this situation, is not tolerated.

I ask you: Is it true that sexism is more accepted than racism?

I cannot be sure. I do not have access to all the data. Still, my observations include seeing women verbally abused by their boyfriends, women mistreated at car repair shops, and more.

What do you see?

And I wonder about questions like: Do women get paid less than men of various ethnic backgrounds? The statistics reveal that women get paid only 79 cents per 1 dollar paid to men.

There is a statistic that Asians make 8% less than white men (that's 92 cents per dollar). So, it looks like being an Asian male has advantages.

As I mentioned, Wicca honors the sacred feminine.

The first problem for all of us, men and women, is not to learn, but to unlearn. – Gloria Steinem

Wicca shines the way for religion to embrace and empower women.

What is it going take to make things better for women?

Positive change IS possible. In 1848, Elizabeth Cady Stanton and Lucretia Mott held a conference to gain the right to vote for women. The 19th Amendment to the U.S. Constitution was not ratified until 1920. That's 72 years* of effort until women gained their right to vote in the USA.

Let's continue to speak up and take positive steps forward.

* Historians write about how the 15th Amendment to the Constitution (1870) granted African American men the right to vote. It is reported that the Voting Rights Act of 1965 was necessary so that the majority of African Americans in the South were registered to vote.

Section Two
Be Smart and Knowledgeable #8

Be Careful About Essential Oils

Many witches say, "Only use real essential oils." Some individuals suggest that synthetics are fine. What's the real deal here?

My own opinion is that real essential oils are optimal. Why?

Real Essentials:
- Use real plant essences
- Have the plant energies in the oil
- Can be reliable (if you work with a trustworthy vendor)

Synthetics can have a number of drawbacks:
- Have no plant energies in the oil (a drawback for doing a spell)
- Use chemicals to create the scents

So, what is the real advantage to synthetics? Lower cost.

Warning: Always get food grade oils and talk to your doctor if you are going to use them as medicine. Some oils may interact with medication and cause trouble. Some oils may even cause trouble if you're only using oils.

There's another problem about certain essential oils. I am against animal cruelty, and we find that some people use ambergris oil (from sperm whales) and civet oil (from civets). This bothers me a lot!

It's suggested by some authors that synthetic oils can be used safely in aromatherapy. They hold to the idea that the aroma in synthetics will still trigger the brain in the same way as the real deal.

Is this true? We probably cannot know for certain. Seeing some research studies on this would help.

Whatever you do ... be safe.

Section Two
Be Smart and Knowledgeable #9

The Ant's Tale

The ant's world was ablaze. Flames towered over the ant as it scampered back and forth. I saw the ant in peril on a piece of firewood in my camp fire. With compassion, I placed a stick next to the piece of firewood that was ablaze at one end. The ant rushed onto the stick.

The ant crawled half way up. But then it frantically jumped off the refuge-stick I offered and dashed back toward the flames.

Again, I placed the stick right in front of the ant. This time it got back on the refuge-stick, and I swiftly lifted the stick and placed it on the ground some distance from the camp fire. The ant was safe.

Sometimes we make bad decisions despite God's and Goddess's warnings. The Gods, in their compassion, save us from our own stupidity.

Earlier today, I drove on the freeway. When a large truck

cut me off, I slammed on the breaks. My car slid down the freeway until the wheels regained traction. With fast reflexes and the Gods' grace I was safe!

Sometimes we are given intuitive guidance to go into a new direction, but our fear sends us back toward the flames. Some people stay in a bad marriage or in a bad job because these are the flames they know. Uncertainty seems to be too much to bear.

We, Wiccans, can call upon the Gods to guide us. They are present. They walk beside us on our journey through our lives. (I wrote a book on this: *Goddess Walks Beside You*.)

The Gods try to be as supportive as possible. All we need to do is ask for help and then step forth on the new, better path. (It's better than getting burned.)

Section Two
Be Smart and Knowledgeable #10

What are Some Good Resources for Traditional Witchcraft?

One of my readers asked, "What are some good resources for traditional witchcraft?"

A number of books serve as good resources for one to learn about Traditional Witchcraft.

Here is a list of authors you can read about Traditional Witchcraft.

- Doreen Valiente
- Moonwater SilverClaw (in particular, see my book *The Hidden Children of the Goddess*)
- Raymond Buckland's (*Complete book of Witchcraft*)
- Gerald Brosseau Gardner
- Maxine Sanders
- Deborah Lipp
- Vivianne Crowley

- Stewart Farrar
- Janet Farrar

On the Web
New Wiccan Church (Facebook.com/newwiccanchurch)
Covenant of The Goddess (Cog.org)
GoddessHasYourBack.com

Section Three
Have Energy

"Watch out! On your right!" my sweetheart said, as a car veered into our freeway lane. I swerved to the left—fortunately there was no car immediately in that space!

"Good move. Well done," he said.

At that moment, I resolved to use a "Beacon Spell" before every road trip.

A Beacon Spell is one that helps your car to be easily seen and noticed. This gets people to pay attention to you. So, when another driver tries to merge, he or she *sees* you!

Such a spell helps the Wiccan Badass to guard her own energy. How? If you're afraid that drivers can cause you trouble (ever drive in Los Angeles?), you'll lose energy to fear.

Instead, when I set a Beacon Spell, I stay strong and safe.

As I mentioned earlier, my definition of a Wiccan Badass is someone who does these three things:

- Seizes choices

- Gains knowledge
- Acts decisively

Setting a Beacon Spell is part of my acting decisively What would be good, decisive actions in your life?

Section Three
Have Energy #1

Can Anyone Get Supernatural Powers?

In my workshops and guest appearances in college Comparative Religion classes, people have asked about gaining supernatural powers.

Some people want supernatural power so they can bring their life to a happier and more successful place. I can relate to that. To accomplish positive and powerful results in your life you do *not* need "supernatural powers." Magick is *not* supernatural. At Merriam-Webster.com, *supernatural* is defined as: "Unable to be explained by science or the laws of nature: of, relating to, or seeming to come from magic, a god, etc."

Magick follows the laws of nature. We're *not* asking, in the traditional Christian mode, for God's intervention. In Wicca, witches are marshalling natural power in certain ways. Here's the process (first mentioned in my book *The Hidden Children of the Goddess*):

Intent

To do successful magick, you need to understand several things. First, you must have an intent. You need to know what you want to manifest. I know this sounds simple, but many people just don't think the intent through.

Let's say you want a car. Okay, why do you want a car? Is it to take you to your job? Or is it something you want to have people envy? Hey I don't judge. But if you just say "I want a car" to the universe, you are likely to get that Pinto down the block.

Let's say you just moved to a new area and you need a car to get you around. You want something nice but economical. You don't want a piece of junk that will break down on you every chance it gets. I suggest you go shopping, whether it be on the internet or at a car lot. Get to know what you want and like for your car.

When you pick out features, you're attaching specific desires to the car. This will help manifest the car you want versus the junk heap down the block. Refine your image of the perfect car in your mind. Include other requirements you have like good gas mileage and inexpensive repair costs. The more specific you are with your intent, the less there will be unexpected results like getting the lemon down the lane.

Having a solid intent is your first step before you do any magick. Once you have that cornerstone set you can continue with the second thing which is concentration. During your spell, you will need lots of concentration and visualization.

Visualization

We'll continue with the process of manifesting a particular car. You can use a toy car as a visualization focus object. As you stare at the toy car, you also use your mind to imagine getting into a real car and driving it. You can even take several steps further. For instance, if you desire a convertible car, you imagine the wind blowing through your hair as you drive with the top down.

Concentration

This is the process of focusing and then refocusing your mind on your visualization task. In essence, you concentrate on the object and on the images in your mind that are specific for your desired manifestation. It is natural for the mind to wander at times. When it does, you just consciously redirect your mind to focus on the visualization object once again.

Meditation

Some Wiccans begin with meditation to clear the mind before using both concentration and visualization. (I share the Tree of Life Meditation in Chapter 9 of my book, *The Hidden Children of the Goddess*.) Once you have cleansed your energy via some form of meditation, you will focus on a shape—that is, a mental image of a shape (perhaps, a pyramid or sphere). Using your mind's eye, view the shape from every angle. Concentrate on this shape for an extended time.

Willpower

The Collins English Dictionary defines willpower as "the ability to control oneself and determine one's actions."

Kelly McGonigal, Ph.D., author of *The Willpower Instinct*, wrote: "Willpower is about harnessing the three powers of I will, I won't and I want to help you to achieve your goals (and stay out of trouble)."

When it comes to successfully performing magick, willpower, to me, means the driving force of desire for some form of change. So, I focus on the power of "I will." This is an important distinction because many people think of willpower as only the ability to avoid temptation.

The compelling observation is that Wiccans, who become proficient at these three processes of visualization, concentration, and meditation, actually strengthen their will. How? Once you do the three processes, you enhance your belief, and you push through your doubt.

Realize, you need to will something into being. This includes confidence that what you are doing will work. If you don't have that, your spell just won't become a reality.

You need your will for your intent to be as strong as possible. This is why when we are desperate for something, we can usually manifest it. Using your will is deeply rooted in your desire. Lack of will just creates another belly flop.

I've now shared with you the five must-haves (intent, visualization, concentration, meditation, and willpower) for doing magick that works.

Now, let's talk about some of the other tools we use to manifest our desires.

When you start to create a spell, you begin with the intent. Once you have that strongly in place, you start crafting the wording of the spell. Be specific, and in this way, you will avoid loopholes or misunderstandings in your magick. Vague wording leads to mistakes and disappointment. Remember, if you merely ask for a car, you might get one that is a piece of junk.

Another tool for working magick is using herbs that attract a particular thing or effect. For example, to attract money, Wiccans often use cinnamon. They also use sage for purifying spaces, people, and more.

I would suggest keeping things simple, at least to start with. Simple spells can be the most potent because they are easy to do.

An example of a simple technique is to appease the

Younger Self, which can be considered one's inner child. The Feri (Fairy) tradition calls this part of ourselves "Sticky Self." The Younger Self (inner child) likes to play. Younger Self likes song, dance, rhyme, and all the sparkly shiny things in life. She/he likes rattles and other objects which we can use as tools to connect with Younger Self.

Why am I talking about Younger Self? Wiccans use Younger Self as a messenger to the Gods. You need to keep Younger Self's attention so that she/he gets the message right. This may sound silly, but doing things that would keep a five-year-old happy in your magick is a good start. This is one reason why we use feathers, incense, candles, and other tools in our magick. There are other reasons, too. Everything has its own energy and meaning. Such energy and meaning help you focus and add power to the work that you do. Don't forget this is work. It takes a lot of energy and concentration to do spell work and magick in general.

So, you have your intent and your words in rhyme. You have added other elements to make Younger Self happy and to lend extra meaning/power to your magick. At this point, once you have gathered all that you need, you cast circle. Do the spell by using your items to focus on your intent. Chant your words and use a power-raising technique (all while keeping keen concentration on your intent).

The next step is important. Without this step, you might as well not have done all the previous efforts. What step am I talking about? You need to let all that energy you raised and all that focus go. That's right, you need to release it into the universe so that it can do the job you set it out to do. This lets Younger Self carry your message to the Gods and to create the change you desire.

* * *

So, as you can see, witches have special ways to work with magick. We use the natural energies around us to create change with Will, Intent, Visualization, Concentration, and Meditation.

Moonwater SilverClaw

Section Three
Have Energy #2

The Blessing of "Speed Grounding"

"What do you recommend for a Wiccan to feel better and to step out of feeling anxious?" a friend asked.

"Meditation," I replied.

Her face dropped. A number of people do not welcome meditation, and many say they do not have the time.

I have developed what I call "Speed Grounding."

As you visualize that you're sending roots into the ground from your feet, say this chant aloud.

Speed Grounding Chant

That which lies in my body deep,
I surrender now through my feet.
Casting down, all my pain to sleep,
Mother Earth, my cares, does she keep.

Now up and up from Her sweet care,
Loving energy She does share.
A cloak of serenity I now wear.

As you repeat the chant, be sure to practice deep breathing.

Section Three
Have Energy #3

A Spell to Attract New and Positive Friends

One of my readers asked about how to create a spell to attract new friends.

I think the easiest spell you can do is a candle spell. Candle spells can be quite simple and yet powerful.

Please read the spell all the way through so you can get an idea of what is happening at each step.

When doing the spell, simply hold onto the feelings of truly wanting good friends to surround you.

Note: Chime candles work well for this spell. Otherwise, you can use tea lights.

What you will need:
- Three Pink candles
- One load stone (you can use a simple magnet if you

do not have one)
- One white candle
- Rose oil or you can use simple olive oil
- Pen and virgin paper (Virgin simply means unused or brand new and un marked and untouched)
- Lighter

Set up:

Write the attributes of what you want in your new friends on the paper. Think of all the wonderful friends you will be attracting.

Place the paper down and put the load stone on top of the paper. Carve your name on the white candle and rub oil on the candle from tip to base. Then place the candle in the middle of the paper next to the load stone.

Carve the word "Friend" on each of the pink candles and rub the oil onto the candle from tip to base. Place the three pink candles in a triangle around the load stone and white candle.

What to do:

Light the white candle and say:

One, two, three, I call out to thee!

Drop a drop of wax from the white candle onto the load stone. Next light one of the pink candles and say:

Lord of Life and my Lady of the Moon,
I ask of you now this simple boon.

Place a drop of wax from the pink candle onto the load stone. Next light the next pink candle, going around clockwise and say:

My desires are simple, and there true,
Bring me friends so loyal, true, and new.

Place a drop of wax from the pink candle onto the load stone. Next light the last pink candle, going around clockwise and say:

Lord of Life and my Lady of the Moon,
Bring me friends healthy, sane and in tune.

Place another drop of wax from the first pink candle onto the load stone. Say:

By the powers of the sun, moon, and sea,
In a fortnight for me to now see.
So mote it be.

Let the candles burn all the way down.
Carry the loadstone in your pocket or purse.
Blessings to you.

Section Three
Have Energy #4

Forgiveness of Yourself on the Path of Joy

Is there a Wiccan path to joy?
What is joy really? Is it happiness?
Not really. It is a step to happiness. Recently, I had the opportunity to hear a talk by Chade-Meng Tan, author of *Joy On Demand*, who said: "Joy is a moment to moment feeling. It is the building block of happiness."

The question is: How do we get to joy? Much of my life I wanted to feel joyful, but various things held me down: a brother who terrorized me and later, an abusive marriage.

I learned a number of things that helped me get stronger, and through Wicca I left that abusive marriage.

Still, how does joy pertain to Wicca?

The Gods want us to be happy.

But many times, we get in our own way. We put shame and anger in our way. What do I mean about that?

We put ourselves down, and we ignore our true beauty and talent. This puts a roadblock to our joy and happiness.

Can you relate to this? Have you ever been mad at yourself for making mistakes or "not being good enough? Or smart enough?"

As I was growing up, having dyslexia, I felt stupid. I had terrible trouble reading and struggled to keep up in school. More than that, I felt that I didn't measure up to the media's idea of feminine beauty. That was a lot of pressure! (Models don't even measure up to it. That's why they are significantly Photoshopped!)

With so much self-directed emotional turmoil, I failed to see myself as the Gods saw me. Beautiful and sacred. It wasn't until I did the *Self Love Meditation* (find it on my blog at http://bit.ly/2fSTvid) that I truly understood this.

With tears in my eyes, I saw the truth.

Now I look to the little things of life to give me joy. For example, a simple drink of water. 783 million people do not have access to clean water. I think of how fortunate I am to have clean water on tap. Taking a drink of water gives me a simple joy.

When's the last time you were thankful and joyful about something? Was it months, weeks, days ago? Think about it. Do you thank the Gods for positive things in your life?

The Gods want us to be happy and have joy in this world. Remember, the Gods are love.

Still, how does self-forgiveness fit in with being a true Wiccan? Picture this. You make a mistake. You get mad at yourself. All you're now looking at is the mistake and how "bad" you were. In effect, you're turning away from what the God and the Goddess want you to see and to nurture. They want you to nurture yourself and have a healthy relationship with yourself. And with such a healthy relationship, you can have a healthy, loving relationship with Them.

Imagine this. How about being compassionate toward yourself? Wouldn't you give a close friend the benefit of the doubt? Wouldn't you be kind to your friend?

How about extending such understanding and kindness to yourself? Forgive yourself for making mistakes. Nurture yourself as you do better and better on your Wiccan path.

Being compassionate is being one with kindness. Kindness is linked to love.

We are of the Gods and the Gods are of us. Forgiving yourself and making room for you to pay attention to joy will empower you. As you experience joy, you naturally bring joy to others as well.

And then the God and Goddess will smile with you in this present moment.

Section Three
Have Energy #5

A Prayer for Healing from a Cold

If you're not feeling well, I feel real empathy for what you're enduring. I'm holding on through my own difficulties with a cold at this moment.

So here is a prayer to help speed your healing.

Light a candle and recite:

When the fever takes hold, may the Gods loosen its grip.
When the chills come over me, may the Gods warm me gently from within.
When the aches and pains torment my body, may the Gods relieve me.
I ask now for Your strength and the healing, Gods! May Your healing be swift and complete unto me.
So mote it be.

May you be happy and well.

Section Three
Have Energy #6

A Source of Peace

Patrick, a Wiccan elder, has a peaceful demeanor. I'd like some of that. Wouldn't you? Perhaps, you've endured some tough times. Wicca, for example, strengthened me so I could leave an abusive marriage.

How is experiencing peace a way to "have energy"? When you're in a peaceful state of being, you are NOT leaking energy. Feeling distracted or upset drains your personal energy. Instead, *feeling peaceful enhances your personal energy.*

What's one way to have a big change of perspective and to acquire some inner peace? Connect with trees. I mean it. Take a walk in a wooded area and breathe easily. Notice if you're drawn to a particular tree. Use the ancient Wiccan greeting for communicating with a tree: Shaminah-Gidoff-Gidow. [I have typed this phonetically.] When you say this phrase out loud, you're telling the tree that you wish it ever flowing water. This is the proper greeting to the tree.

Hold your hands out and on the trunk or limb of the tree. Open your heart and mind. Reach out to the tree with them. Then listen.

You may get feelings, pictures, words, or whole sentences.

When you're done, leave a gift for the tree. You could give the tree water or bury crystals near it. (Make sure your gift is biodegradable and that it won't hurt the tree.)

You can even meditate under the tree. Remember: Always thank the tree.

Try and establish a relationship with the tree. Visit weekly to talk, listen and leave a small gift.

Section Three
Have Energy #7

Blockage Release Ritual

Some people have a blockage to receiving money or love.
This following Blockage Release Ritual often helps dissolve that which block your highest good.

You will need:
- An object that represents the blockage in your life
- A red string or piece of yarn long enough so you can both encircle your waist and then tie to "blockage object" to you. Have at least one foot of length between you and the object.
- A boline and other ritual tools. (See my blog article at http://bit.ly/1Pheqpz for more information.)

1) Cast Your Circle
(See http://bit.ly/1Pheqpz again for more information.)

2) Begin the Ritual

Asperge the "blockage object." (Asperge means to sprinkle the holy water onto the object with your fingers.)

As you asperge the object say:

I cleanse and consecrate you by water and earth.

Cense the object. (Cense means to waft incense smoke over the object.)

As you cense the object, say:

I bless and charge you with air and fire.
Asperge the yarn/string while you say:
I cleanse and consecrate you by water and earth.
Cense the yarn/string as you say,
I bless and charge you with air and fire.

Take the red yarn/string in your hands, and say:

Tiny bundle of yarn/string, you are now the same as the bonds between me and [Name of Blockage].

Tie one end of the yarn/string to the object and then encircle your waist with the other end of the yarn/string, while you say:

You are the bonds that connect us now.
From me to [Name of blockage] and from [Name of blockage] to me.
Our connection is by thee.

Sit and concentrate on the bond between you both and see it as the yarn/string that now connects you and the object.

Once you have that idea firmly in mind, use the boline to cut the yarn/string, while you see, in your mind's eye, the astral bonds being cut along with the yarn/string.

Once you complete the cut, say:

I am now free of the ties of [Name of blockage] as it is of me.
May my happiness expand on the count of three.
One
Two
Three
Blessed be.

3) Do the Cakes and Wine Ceremony
4) Close Your Circle

Section Three
Have Energy #8

Take Back the Power of the Pentagram

"It bothers me that some films and television shows use the pentagram to symbolize 'the bad guys' or simply 'the occult,'" my friend Allison said.

"We know the truth. We know that the pentagram is the main symbol of Wicca. It represents the Goddess, life and the elements," I replied.

All Five Elements are represented by each point on the pentagram as seen on the next page:

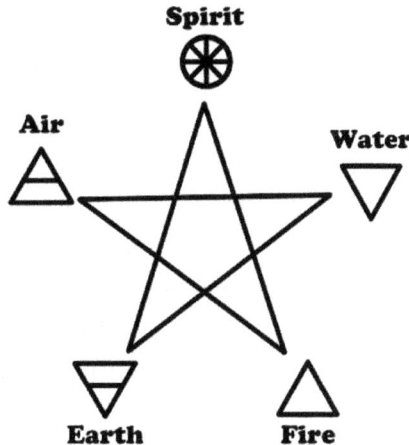

Every being from humans to cats (for example) has the Five Elements as part of his or her makeup.

Air represents the direction East.

The sun rises in the East. Associated with the time of dawn, air belongs during the morning. East means new beginnings. So, anything that begins or "dawns" is of the Air symbol. Air represents thought, and new ideas dawn in our heads all the time. East is a male element. This is not to say that females don't have the Air element in them. Still, Wiccans consider Air to be a masculine.

Air reflects thought and intelligence. Simply put, Air is pure thought. We use the attributes of Air to figure out our problems. The skill of problem solving is Air's strength. Think of math and science as subjects ruled by Air.

Things that represent Air are feathers/birds of all kinds, clouds, dust devils, wind chimes, and incense smoke to name a few.

The sylph is the Elemental of Air. Some artists have depicted sylphs as human figures with wings. Sylphs are often seen in cloud formations. Note that an Elemental is an entity that embodies one specific element.

In many Tarot decks, swords represent Air. Since Air is the element of thought and intellect, Tarot swords represent ideas and other qualities of Air. But just like a real sword, thoughts can cut two ways. They can be freeing or debilitating, just as having a life-altering epiphany is to having depression.

Fire represents the direction South.

Fire is associated with noon, the hottest time of the day. As with Air, Fire is a masculine element. Fire is action! Fire represents your will. It is the spark that sets you into motion. It is the energy that moves you to finish your housework.

Fire is represented by embers, the sun, hot chili peppers, and a flame from a candle.

Salamanders are the Elemental spirits of Fire. The Fire salamander is seen as dragon-like. Like flames, they are shape-shifters. They are sometimes depicted with wings and human faces, much like sylphs.

In many Tarot decks, wands represent Fire. Whereas Air is the beginning or the plan you start with, Fire sets that plan into action!

Fire also transforms. It changes whatever it touches, consuming it and converting it into something new. The Phoenix is a good example of this. It is consumed by fire and then rises from its own ashes as something new. In a sense, it is being reborn out of its own destruction.

Water represents the direction West.

Water's corresponding time of day is at sunset. Water is associated with the moon and with birth, death, and rebirth. It also has to do with feelings and emotions. Water connotes strong feelings such as love, desire, hate, joy, and sorrow. Water is a feminine element. Things that represent water are seashells, seaweed, water, sponges, and fish.

Because of its association with death, Water is also associated with the Summerlands (afterlife). Many folkloric traditions include a journey over a body of water to reach their afterlife.

The Undine is the Elemental spirit in water. Undines are water entities that can manifest themselves in many forms, from mermaids to the sirens of the sea.

In many Tarot decks, cups represent Water. In Tarot, cups represent emotions. Cups are also associated with birth, death, and rebirth.

You may recall that my name is Moonwater SilverClaw. I chose this name because I feel connected to water. My mother still tells tales of how, as a child, I'd find any puddle in a two-mile radius. To this day I enjoy the water whether I'm snorkeling or doing undersea helmet diving.

Earth represents the direction North.

Midnight is the time that is associated with this element. Earth stands for stability, foundations, and commitment. The greatest image of Earth is Mother Earth or Gaia herself. Earth is a feminine element. Earth is also stillness. Earth is represented by rocks, crystals, dirt, and fossils.

Gnomes are the Elemental spirits of Earth. Gnomes are strong and squat. Their skin is the colors of the Earth with its many shades of brown to black.

In many Tarot decks, Earth is represented by coins or pentacles. Coins in the Tarot connote physical labors and the fruits of those labors. They often refer to physical possessions, such as money, cars, and houses.

Spirit does not have a specific direction or a specific time in our twenty-four-hour day. That being said, Spirit is what creates the life within us. It is literally the divine spark that we all need to be alive. There is no Elemental associated with Spirit.

What we call the "soul" is in fact a piece of the God and Goddess, or "The All." Every one of us has this element within us. It is the element that makes all living things divine.

This above recipe creates a whole living being.

Think of it: We even have the Five Elements in ourselves as a microcosm.

Water is our blood which contains 85% of the salt in the human body. In a way, our blood has similarities to ocean water. Fire manifests as the body heat that arises from glucose produced by the liver. Earth is the solid body—the bones and flesh. Air fills our lungs. Spirit animates all of the elements into the living being you are.

You need the Elements of earth, air, water and fire to create a vessel for the spirit to reside.

The pentagram is the representative blueprint for life, and the pentagram represents the Goddess.

You will notice that the pentagram is in the shape of a human—and more than that, it represents the Sacred Feminine. Our ancestors understood that life came from the Sacred Feminine. We are all born from mothers. Woman is the place where life is created. So, if you're a woman be proud of the fact that you are a representative of the Goddess.

Section Three
Have Energy #9

How Do You Pick the Right Coven for You?

One of my readers asked, "How do you pick the right coven for you?"

That can be a complicated topic. Here I'll share three helpful methods.

1. **Devote some time with the coven members in a casual setting.**

Look at getting together for coffee (or another beverage). Have some casual conversations and note how you feel when you're in the presence of the coven members. Are you comfortable? After the get-together, do you feel good? Energized?

Or was your experience somehow different? Did you feel like you just didn't mesh with a number of the coven members? Did they somehow look down upon you for being too much of a "newbie" — or something else?

2. Watch how coven members interact with each other.

Do they treat each other with respect? Is there bickering among some coven members? You're looking for a safe and uplifting environment. Even if you're "desperate" to join a coven, you might find that a specific coven is not (at the moment) a healthy place for you. You might even be triggered (that is, something from your past may be rising up. Someone may be acting in a cruel way like your sibling did when you were younger).

3. Observe whether it is too hard to get to the coven's meeting place.

Covens work when members can consistently attend ritual. If it's too hard to get to the meeting place, particularly if you've had a draining week, you might miss some gatherings.

Also, pay attention to whether the meetings run late and whether you can be safe on your way home (if you take public transportation).

Ultimately, joining a coven is for uplifting your soul. Be careful and keep looking for a good match.

Section Four
Make Things Happen

Just before I fell asleep, I expressed my intention. "God and Goddess, please help me find the perfect car. It will be dark blue in color. It'll have a rear camera for parking. There will be a USB port. It's a Toyota car with low mileage. It will be a used car but a recent year. I can afford the price."

I went to sleep feeling good, knowing that I had been specific in my intention.

The next day, I went looking and ... Boom! The perfect car. It was the *same year model*. Somehow, someone had purchased the car and returned it in just a couple of months. It only had 9,000 miles on it. Unbelievable!

So I bought it.

As I mentioned earlier, my definition of a Wiccan Badass is someone who does these three things:

- Seizes choices
- Gains knowledge
- Acts decisively

Yes—I acted decisively to get my dark blue Toyota car. This section will help you take action.

Section Four
Make Things Happen #1

Moonwater SilverClaw's Formula for Making a Spell

"I really could use a simple format for making a spell, Moonwater," my friend Anita said.

"Okay. I can give you the basics with a 5-Step Formula for Making a Spell," I replied.

It comes down to these steps or what I call the "5 What's":
- What do you want?
- What element?
- What will represent that element?
- What do you have at hand?
- What words?
- What do you want?

Seems simple enough, right? Still, many people hold the thought "I want more money." That's too vague. What do you want the money for? Some people have a job that pays well enough but they hate that job. So, what do they do? They buy expensive stuff and vacations. Perhaps, what they really want is a job that they feel good about.

Now, ask yourself: *What do I want?* Then ask yourself, *What do I <u>really</u> want?* Keep refining it until you have it. Finding the root of the need is important.

What element?
How do you pick the appropriate element? Think about your need. What element is connected to it?

- Do you want to flow better at work? That relates to Water.
- Do you want to think more clearly? That's related to the element Air.
- If you want more energy, you likely want to connect with the spark—with Fire.
- Do you feel scattered? To connect with being grounded, focus on Earth.

Questions like these will help you pick what element is best suited for your problem or desire.

What will represent that element?
What object would make a good representation of your element? If it's Fire, perhaps, a lit candle. If it's water, you could use a sea shell because it comes from the sea.

What do you have at hand?
With a list of objects that can represent your element, see what you have on hand that would fit the bill. Perhaps your first thought was to use a shell as part of your spell. However, you do not have one in your home. You could simply grab a bowl and fill it with water.

What words?
The words you choose are important.
Here are three details to help you.

Choose an opening
Here's an example:
By the powers of the Sun and Moon

Give a deadline
Here's an example:
So make this happen nine days or less

Put in the protection phrases
Here is an example:
An it harm none.

I also include "This or better." There are times when the God and Goddess know better than we do what would be good for our overall journey of life.

Additionally, give a time period for the spell to stop. You can say something like: *May it come to pass within three moons.* (Spells usually come to pass within one moon cycle.)

May the above details help you in forming your spell. It's true that one may add other details to a spell. Still, the above provides you with a good start.

The various parts of your spell are like the pieces you put together when sewing a quilted blanket.

Section Four
Make Things Happen #2

Should I Create Spells or Follow a Book?

One of my readers asked, "Should I create spells or follow a book?"

The real answer is "both." Reading a book can give you the format for different forms of spells. In my books, including *The Hidden Children of the Goddess*, I show the specific actions and scripts to say. After you learn the format, you can customize the spell.

The Strongest Spells Are Ones You Create Personally

Reading books is a good start. But I suggest the strongest spells are ones you make yourself. Just because a spell is in a book doesn't mean that it's the right spell for the job at hand.

However, you can use the previous section *Moonwater SilverClaw's Formula for Making a Spell* as a springboard. It is just a template for a beginning.

The Value of Customizing Your Spell

Here are the benefits you gain from customizing your spell:

- Creating your own spells is a good way of learning the ropes.
- You gain a better grasp of the fundamentals in Wicca as a spiritual path.
- You become a better practitioner.
- You tailor the spell to you and your unique situation.

Remember to include a protection phrase like "An it harm none."

Section Four
Make Things Happen #3

Composing Your Words for Your Spell

Often, in my enewsletter, I provide chants and prayers.
Readers noticed that I use rhymes.
Why? There is a power in the music and rhythm associated to the words.
I invite you to try your hand at putting some words together.
Over the years, I find that certain combinations of words just sound better to me.
Recently, a friend asked me, "How do you do it? Put rhymes in your chant or prayer."
"You just ask for what you want in a rhyming, poetic way," I replied.
So, it all begins with a positive desire.
I begin with the concept.
Here's an example of a portion of a Money Spell from my blog at

Goddesshasyourback.com/2016/02/19/money-prosperity-and-wiccans-enjoying-life-a-money-spell/

As I light this candle so,
Make my money grow and grow,
Let it flow without rhyme or reason,
Each and every turn of season,
Filling up my pockets so wide,
Let me enjoy this happy ride,
Make me stronger than the ocean tides,
Manifesting my will to coincide,
With no malice, woe, or hitches,
May there be no mess or jinxes,
With no need of fear of ruin,
Let it rain money, bless my journey.
An it harm none, so mote it be!

The pattern you see above is the use of a couplet (defined as "a literary device which has two successive rhyming lines in a verse" – from LiteraryDevices.net)

You might want to start with couplets because putting them together may feel easier.

Discover how your spells feel more powerful as you use rhymes.

Section Four
Make Things Happen #4

How Do You Put Together a Ritual?

"I want my ritual to be special," Melinda said.

"It all begins with focusing on the right questions and then coming up with your own answers," I replied.

As you put a ritual together, begin with these following questions:
- What is the ritual for?
- What do you need (items) for the ritual?
- How many people are going to be there?
- Does anyone have food allergies? (Cakes and Wine Ceremony)
- Is it going to be indoors or outdoors?
- When is it to be held? (phases of the moon or time of day needed)
- Will people need to bring anything?
- What mood and flavor are you trying to inspire? (Is this a celebratory ritual?)

- Is your ritual going to be a solemn funeral? Or a joyful handfasting (Wiccan wedding)?

Think about what items you will need. Acquire all items in advance.

Make sure you ask about the participants' food allergies. You don't want to have to call the paramedics in the middle of your ritual.

If you consider holding your ritual outdoors, check on the weather forecast. Still, plan for what to do if it does rain unexpectedly.

Timing for your ritual effects the outcome. Check your calendar for the best time for the work you will be doing.

Will your participants need to bring an offering or something else to your ritual? Give them time to prepare in advance.

Think of your ritual as being similar to pulling together a recipe. You bring together the ingredients. When you put together the recipe well and you follow it, you'll create a joyful experience for your ritual attendees.

Section Four
Make Things Happen #5

What Could Possibly Make Magick or Spells Fail to Work for Someone?

Many times, a person may block the spell unknowingly because human beings tend to build emotional walls around themselves. Such walls are blocks that keep one stuck. This is an unconscious process. We need to unblock ourselves and tear down these walls.

Here is an example. Sarah does a money spell because her stated goal is: "I want to be rich." The spell fails to work. She sits down to do a meditation session. She asks, "What is blocking me?" During the meditation, images and sounds arise. She sees, in her mind's eye, a gathering in which she and friends say biased things against rich people. On the subconscious level, Sarah and her friends feel "more spiritual" than rich people. This unconscious block stops Sarah from enhancing her income. On the subconscious level, she does not want to join the "less spiritual," rich people.

The truth is: a significant number of people have a subconscious "counter-desire" that blocks their progress.

Sarah learns to develop a willingness to let go of her biased viewpoints about "rich people." She realizes that she can be kind and generous at any time. She can trust that as her income grows, she can continue to be kind and generous.

Some months ago, I did a workshop about removing these forms of blocks.

It's true that it can take work to let go and remove blocks.

It's worth it.

Section Four
Make Things Happen #6

Dedicating Your Labors to the Gods

Perspiration dripping from my face, my ankles shaking due the rocky trail, I gasped for breath. Two miles into this hike, and I had a good idea: I'd dedicate my journey on this trail to the Gods. I offered my hard work as a gift to them. You can make such an offering with many things. Still, a struggle has a special element. When you struggle, you put more energy into the activity. The God and Goddess appreciate such devotion of energy.

Upon hearing about this process of dedicating my hike, my friend Sandra said, "That sounds like the Catholic idea of 'offering up one's suffering."

"No," I protested. "The Gods don't want your suffering. They want you to be happy." I explained. In *The Charge of the Goddess*, author Doreen Valiente noted the Voice of the Goddess saying: "All acts of love and pleasure are My rituals."

You can do many things to honor the Gods. Some suggestions include:
- Create an art project
- Volunteer for an organization, especially one that helps the planet or animals
- Accomplish a physical feat (like my hike)
- Write a book and dedicate it to Them
- Clean your ritual space and altar on a regular basis

Dedicating your labors is a great way to honor the God and Goddess.

Section Four
Make Things Happen #7

How to Stop Self-Sabotaging Your Spells

"It's not working," Sandi said.

"What?" I asked.

"My spells. I know what I want. It's just not manifesting. Why is that?"

"There can be many reasons," I replied.

After an extended conversation, Sandi and I uncovered that her self-doubt and even low self-esteem were sabotaging her efforts.

The truth is: If you do not believe you can make a change, you won't. Self-doubt is the one of the biggest problems we have as practitioners of the Craft.

Recently, I shared a spell to attract new and positive friends. It's not just about doing the ritual according to the steps. If you don't believe you deserve new and positive friends, you may find that the spell falters.

Much of how magick works is on the subconscious level.

If you have been trying and trying to do a spell, and you're not getting what you want, consider looking into what you truly believe.

So how do you get down to the root of the problem—to what you believe on the subconscious level?

Meditation can help here. Meditating on the problem and asking the Gods for help in locating the issue can help you find the problem area(s).

Realize that your subconscious mind speaks in images and metaphors. It may take some time to unravel the mystery.

Some of us would like a shortcut. So, we may buy a dreams-and-symbols book. This will *not* help on the level that I'm talking about. Why? Only you know your own unique symbols.

Here's an example. Sandi finds that a red ball keeps jumping into her thoughts as she meditates. A dreams-and-symbols book may say one thing. But, for Sandi, a red ball means something specific. It takes her a couple of meditation sessions before the memory rises.

During her childhood, Sandi's favorite toy was a red ball. When she was five, Sandi's friend Amanda took that ball away. Not just that. Amanda hit Sandi. That's a painful memory. Additionally, it's reported that much of what we think about the world is formed when we're quite young.

During her meditation, Sandi realizes that the image of the red ball brings a rush of feelings: anger, sadness, and pain over a betrayal. "Amanda was my friend. How could she be so mean?!" Sandi thinks.

To Make Your Spells Work, You May Need to Work with Deep-Seated Feelings

To find your way to new and healthy friendships, you might need to deal with your deep-seated feelings and beliefs about people. If, on the subconscious level, you feel afraid of being betrayed again, your subconscious mind might be blocking your spellwork. It doesn't want you to get hurt again. You need sit with your feelings, to heal, and to let go.

Several of us find working with a therapist is helpful.

Now, this may be a bit of a disappointment to some Wiccans who are looking for a fast, easy way to solve problems by just casting a spell. We're talking about your whole life here. Our subconscious mind is part of the picture.

Many of us do not want to delve into the unpleasant side of our journey here on earth. Some people just want to focus on "everything that is light and shiny."

I understand that. I can say from personal experience: You can travel further on your path of healing and personal growth when you are willing to look at a hidden side of yourself.

Wicca is a path that helps us connect with who we truly are.

I invite you to welcome the whole experience: joy, recovery, healing, necessary tears and the expansion and enhanced ability with spellwork that you're looking forward to.

Section Four
Make Things Happen #8

How to Do an Effective Money Spell

At one point, my family was going through some money difficulties.

I did the following Money Spell, and one of my family members got a new client!

Considering that, here is the Money Spell.

Money Spell

You will need:
- A green candle
- "A check to yourself from the Universe"*
- Cauldron
- Money drawing oil
- Money Oil (add drops of essential oils together)
- 3 parts ginger
- 2 parts orange

- 4 parts pine
- 2 parts cinnamon
- 1/2-part chamomile
- 1 part cedar wood
- 5 parts jasmine (optional)
- matches or a lighter

* We create a check from the Universe by writing the amount we want and writing "from the Universe for the Good of All" in the memo section on the check.

Warning: ONLY work this spell during the waxing moon.

Cast Circle in the usual manner.

Dress the green candle properly. (That is, dab your finger in the money oil and rub the candle repeatedly from wick to base—until the whole candle is covered in money oil.)

As you dress the candle, envision money flowing into your life.

Light the candle and chant the following out loud:

As I light this candle so,
Make my money grow and grow,
Let it flow without rhyme or reason,
Each and every turn of season,
Filling up my pockets so wide,
Let me enjoy this happy ride,
Make me stronger than the ocean tides,
Manifesting my will to coincide,
With no malice, woe or hitches,

May there be no mess or jinxes,
With no need of fear of ruin,
Let it rain money, bless my journey.
An it harm none, so mote it be!

Now hold the "Check from the Universe." Light the check via the candle and place the check in the cauldron to burn safely.

Watch the flame as it burns the check.

Meditate while focusing on the flame of the green candle.

When you are ready, place the green candle in a safe place and let the candle burn completely out. [Do NOT leave an unattended candle. Stay safe.]

Enjoy the Cakes and Wine Ceremony
Close the Circle.

Section Four
Make Things Happen #9

How to Mix Oils and Make Sprays to Enhance Your Magick

You can choose from an assortment of different oils to use in magick. Wiccans use oils to anoint candles, sachets, talismans, amulets, crystals, and people. You can also wear oils like perfumes.

An oil's scent creates energy, which we use in our magick.

Make sure that the oils you use are genuine and authentic essential oils—in other words, that they are made from the plants themselves. The plant's oils carry the plant's properties and energies that we use in our magick. Many distributors will slap on the label "essential oil" to make a buck, but many of these are synthetic scents, which do *not* carry a plant's vital energies or properties. For this you need genuine oils that come directly from the plant itself.

Undiluted oils can irritate your skin. So, dilute them by adding them to a base oil. To do this, take 1/8 cup of a base oil such as Jojoba oil. Then, using an eye dropper, place around 9 drops of the undiluted essential oil into your base oil. Swirl in a clockwise direction to mix. Then you can use this mixture on the skin for anointing.

To anoint the body, rub your diluted oil mixture on your wrists, neck, and sometimes behind the knees if desired. This will let your body absorb the energies of the oils.

Magickal Sprays

For people who have difficulties being around the smoke of incense, using magickal sprays may be a good solution. Sprays also help when one lives in a building with rules against the use of incense.

Several Wiccans consider sprays to be a new invention and *not* part of traditional witchcraft.

Up to now, I have not used sprays. But when one of my readers asked about them, I took an interest and looked into what some Wiccans do.

Use a glass spray bottle and avoid plastic because plastic can leach into your solution making it tainted.

Dark colored glass bottles protect the oils within.

Start with spring water or, if necessary, you can use distilled water. Pour water to fill your glass atomizer spray bottle up to its shoulder.

Drop three or nine drops (or a combination of your oils) of each oil into your spray bottle.

Warning: *Do not place stones or crystals in your bottles due to the fact that some type of harmful trace elements may be within such crystals or stones. (I learned this from a geologist.) Some trace elements can make you quite ill or worse.*

If you want to add the energies of stones to your spray,

you can use this safe method: Nestle the bottle of finished magickal spray in a small basin filled with your chosen stone.

If you only have one crystal or stone, you can fill the basin with water and set the item in the basin. Place the basin into the light of the full moon.

Warning: *Make sure that your bottle is tightly sealed so that your contents are safely separated from the water contained in the basin.*

May your spells be enhanced.

Section Four
Make Things Happen #10

Ritual for Healing

"I'm so concerned about my friend, Rose," a reader, Julie, told me in a chat-conversation.

During our conversation, Julie said that she wanted to do a ritual of healing for Rose. I first made sure to ask if Rose had given Julie the permission to do a healing ritual on her behalf. Julie said, "Yes."

Here is the Ritual for Healing

What you will need:
- A photo of the person needing to be healed
- 5 pieces of rose quartz
- 5 small clear quartz crystals
- 1 green candle
- Candle holder
- Healing oil (olive oil that has been blessed will do)

- Your normal ritual tools

What to do:
Cast circle as usual.

Cleanse and consecrate all the crystals, the candle, picture, and the rose quartz. Take the green candle and dress* it, placing it in its holder.

Arrange the quartz and rose quartz crystals in an alternating pattern in a circle—around the candle. Light the candle.

Pick up the green candle (be careful) and hold it, facing the East, and say:

Let the power of East and illuminate my intention for healing for "Name of Sick Person." May his/her ailment flee from "Name of Sick Person" like a gentle breeze. May the Goddess breathe healing into "Name of Sick Person."

Still holding the green candle, now walk to the cardinal point of the South, and say:

Let the power of South ignite my intention for healing for "Name of Sick Person." May his/her ailment abate from "Name of Sick Person" and take fever from his/her body. May the Goddess's bright spirit show "Name of Sick Person" the way to full health.

Still holding the green candle, now walk to the cardinal point of the West, and say:

Let the power of West rise up and let my intention wash the sickness of "Name of Sick Person" away. May his/her ailment evaporate like water in the Sun. May the Goddess's healing flow to "Name of Sick Person."

Still holding the green candle, now walk to the cardinal

point of the North and say:

Let the power of North give my intention a steady place to heal the sickness of "Name of Sick Person" away. May his/her ailment crumble like earth, revealing healthy new growth—the green of grass and life. May the Goddess fully heal "Name of Sick Person."

Take the green candle back to the circle of quartz and place the photo in the center. Now to facilitate the healing energy to go into the person, place the candle holder (with candle) upon the photo.

Sit and meditate on seeing the person healthy and well. See the person walking and laughing with friends.

When you are finished meditating, thank all the powers that helped in the healing.

Do the Cakes and Wine Ceremony.

Close Circle in the usual way (while you make sure to dismiss the Elements).

Please be sure that the candle burns down complete. Be sure to never leave a burning candle unattended. Stay safe.

*To dress the candle means: The process of putting your desire into the candle. As you clearly envision your wish, rub anointing oil (olive oil will suffice) on the candle. Spread the oil from the top of the candle to the center, and then from the bottom back to the center. Rubbing from each end of the candle to the center draws or attracts a desire to you. If you wish to repel something, for example an illness or bad luck, you would rub from the center out to each end of the candle. This pushes away what you wish to repel.

Section Five
Protect Yourself

"Moonwater, I'm so glad you're here!" Molly said, as she invited me into her home.

She had asked me to do a house blessing to remove the negative energy left as a residue from her previous roommate.

A Wiccan Badass takes care of herself and her surroundings.

Your home should feel good energy-wise. It's a place for your renewal which helps you step back out into the world with the swagger of a Wiccan Badass.

Have you noticed that a badass in a movie often has both strength and a calm confidence?

Where does that come from?

This comes from knowing yourself. Meditation and talking to the Gods helps you understand who you are.

In knowing yourself, you realize your great worth bestowed by the Gods. So, you want to protect this gift.

The Wiccan Badass protects herself.

Remember, you can't give what you don't have.

You must protect your own energy so that you can move in this world with more confidence and even generosity.

It's likely that you want to give to your friends and family.

Protecting yourself helps you repel things that which would rob you of your necessary and positive energy.

Let's begin …

Section Five
Protect Yourself #1

Guard Your Wiccan Path

I'm 13 years old, and my red hair was a striking gift from my Scottish grandfather. He'd call it a gift. But as I walked past John Gill Elementary School, the bullies (some mean boys) used my red hair as a target of ridicule to smash my self-esteem.

Day after day, they teased me.

What was I to do? Would I dye it purple? Would I hide it beneath a baseball cap?

Actually, I wasn't thinking of hiding my hair at all. Instead, I wished that *I did not have* red hair.

The teasing caused a whirlwind of anger to rise up in my chest until it was a full-fledged storm of fury. I ran toward the fence and kicked it. Then I shook that fence. The boys just laughed at me from the safety of the other side.

But then something shifted in my thinking. There's got to be another way I can walk home from school. So, I found another way to walk home. I finally got those boy's taunts out of my life.

Today, I was talking with a friend about walking our Wiccan Path.

As Wiccans, we often must walk a path that includes the taunts of non-Wiccans. These people, fueled by lies in the entertainment media, are misinformed and uneducated. Like those boys, they are NOT worth our time.

Whatever you do, avoid letting yourself fall into a trap of failing to honor your own spiritual truth.

I understand that, as a 13-year-old, I wanted to *not* have red hair—a target of teasing.

Still, now as a woman, I know that I am strong enough to *own* my red hair and my Wiccan Path.

I invite you to consider how you can gather with like-minded people.

You can enjoy your path home.

Section Five
Protect Yourself #2

Protection, the Insta-circle

Use this in emergencies against bad energies. It's quick and can save you from negative forces.

While you say this chant, trace a circle three times around yourself deosil (clockwise) sending out energy around you.

Chant:
I now cast the circle round, round and round!
I'm now thrice protected from head to ground!

Section Five
Protect Yourself #3

Fairies, Shadow People and Spirits—Oh My!

Out of the corner of my eye, I saw a shape. Wispy. Dark-tinted but see through. Sort of an outline. Then it was gone. I saw these shapes about five times in a house I used to live in. Ghosts? No. They're called Shadow People. One of my mentors gave me some information about the Shadow People. An important distinction is that Shadow People are spirits that have never been incarnate; they are not ghosts. Shadow People are negative spirits that can engulf people in fear.

I was fortunate. I moved out of that house, and I did not have extreme encounters with the Shadow People.

Warning: *Do NOT contact the Shadow People.*

Recently, one of my readers asked: "How do I contact the Fair Folk?"

There are several ways to contact the Fairies (also known

as The Fey). By the way, Fairies like flowers. If you compliment a flower and say how pretty it is, the associated fairy likes it. Fairies like being complimented for their work.

The most popular method to contact a Fairy is through offerings. A popular offering is honey and milk.

Some fairies prefer a certain element. You can pick a certain offering related to a specific element.

Water – Wine, Juice, Milk
Earth – Incense, Seeds, Crystals/Stones, Dance
Fire – Burn Incense, Burn an offering
Air – Burn Incense, Smoke, Singing, Music

Another powerful way is to meditate with a pure heart and with respect. Ask for a sign. The Fey don't like to be seen.

Some people report that they have actually seen the Fey. If the Fey want you to see them, then they will choose to become visible. But most of the time, they only allow themselves to be seen in your peripheral vision if at all.

When it comes to Fairies, Shadow People and Spirits, be respectful.

Section Five
Protect Yourself #4

Love Spells: About Love and Manipulation

One of my readers asked me, "What do you call the magic power revolving around love and manipulation?"

Love magick and spells are very popular. There are many love spells you can do. You can read my post *The Down and Dirty about Love Spells*

at my blog GoddessHasYourBack.com

It is very important to NOT manipulate another person.

So here I want to separate the topics "love" and "manipulation."

First, let's take a look at love. I appreciate these quotes:

"Love is friendship that has caught fire. It is quiet understanding, mutual confidence, sharing and forgiving. It is loyalty through good and bad times. It settles for less than perfection and makes allowances for human weaknesses."

– Ann Landers

"The beginning of love is to let those we love be perfectly themselves, and not to twist them to fit our own image. Otherwise we love only the reflection of ourselves we find in them."
– Thomas Merton

So, if one is interested in having a real love relationship, one would NOT use any form of manipulation.

Why? The Law of Three is very powerful. I wrote about this on this blog:

"I have personally seen Law of Three results unfold in my daily life. The Law of Three holds that we receive three times whatever we send out into the universe.

I've noticed that my actions do bring things in response that are similar in tone.

Do we always get exactly three times the response to an action? Not necessarily.

Imagine that you remove a log from your yard. Likely, some little creatures live in that log. Now homeless, they must find a new place to live. Most often, this might be a small situation.

But what if they were termites and their new home is your house?!

So, a small action (removing the log) led to a big reaction (termite damage). Perhaps, needing to have your home repaired causes you stress.

In this above example, we see that one action may be magnified. How much depends on many variables and how a particular action effects the universe."

* * * * * *

Directing a love spell specifically at one person is unethical. Instead, you can do a spell to remove the blocks to love in yourself. You could also do a spell for you to attract a great match of a love partner.

"Your task is not to seek for love, but merely to seek and find all the barriers within yourself that you have built against it." – Rumi

So, with the above background, let's now be specific.

The question was: "What do you call the magic power revolving around love and manipulation?"

I call magick power that revolves around love ethical.

I call magick power that revolves around manipulation to be unethical AND foolish. Who wants to cause trouble and get three times that trouble thrown back in one's face?!

Be careful out there.

Section Five
Protect Yourself #5

Witches Are Not Pacifists

Would a witch stand by and let a friend get knocked down?

Some people think that *The Wiccan Rede*, by stating "An it harm none," means that witches are pacifists. This is *not* true.

By the way, a definition of "pacifist" emphasizes "a person who believes that war and violence are unjustifiable."

Could a violent act to prevent more violence be justified?

"Witches' morality can be summed up in one sentence, 'Do what you will, so long as it harms none.' This does not mean, however, that witches are pacifists. They say that to allow wrong to flourish unchecked is not 'harming none'. On the contrary, it is harming everybody." – Doreen Valiente

How do we get clear about when we must intervene to prevent more harm?

The following questions apply both to casting spells and our daily actions:

1. Is it personal?

Is this situation about gaining personal vengeance? Wicca is about honoring the God and Goddess—and being in tune with the natural world. Vengeance has no place here.

2. Will this action do more harm or would it prevent additional harm from happening?

My elders have advised that if you can solve a situation without magick, solve it that way.

Let's say you recognized a serial rapist (confirmed by a conviction) running down the sidewalk. If you stuck your foot out to trip him, that would be a type of violence. However, if this serial rapist is not returned to prison, he would assault more people. So, tripping him IS advised—so the police officer trailing him can cuff him.

3. What is at stake here?

Who will be affected by your actions? Remember the effects are ripples in a pond the move out and away from the impact or casting of a spell.

4. What consequences will there be?

Think deeply about what may be the consequences of your casting a spell. The classic example is making a faulty love spell. It is unethical to try to "force" someone to love you. Why? You are acting against that person's will. Many negative consequences can arise including a backlash against you! I'll trust that you do *not* want to have your own will to be thwarted.

5. Who will be affected by these consequences?

Who are all the people involved in the long-term effects of your actions? How will their lives be changed? Make sure you identify the players, the roles they take, and what might happen.

6. Are you willing to pay the price?

All magick creates consequences and even some form of aftermath that is not expected. Whatever you do, you will pay a price. Be careful.

These are some of the questions you need to ask yourself before trying to intervene in some situation.

It is reported that certain witches have cast spells to get rapists convicted and put into prison. That sounds like what Doreen Valiente talked about in making sure to stop "wrong from harming everybody."

Section Five
Protect Yourself #6

Protect Your Energy Related to Toxic Relationships

One of my readers asked, "Do you have any stories of Wiccan spells that were successful?"

I have several stories about successful spells. Here I'll provide an example.

Spell for Separation and an Easier Divorce Process

Years ago, I was in an abusive marriage. I was afraid that in asking for a divorce, I'd open a door to even more pain and trouble.

After I said to myself, "I want a divorce," I did a Separation Ritual. Later, I was surprised how my then-husband gave no trouble and simply signed the divorce papers. What a relief!

Here are the steps of True Separation:
- Verbally end the relationship
- Stay away from the person.
- Ground yourself.
- Cast Circle.
- Do the Separation Ritual (see below).
- Do the Cakes and Wine ritual.
- Close the Circle
- Finally continue to have no contact with the toxic person.

You will need your usual ritual items to cast circle and your altar. As I mentioned you will also have a length of yarn or piece of red string. The yarn/string must be long enough to encircle your own waist and to encircle the object (that represents the toxic person).

The Separation Ritual

Hold the object. In a moment, you will asperge it. (*Asperge* means to sprinkle the holy water with your fingers onto the object.)

With the holy water, asperge and say:
I cleanse and consecrate you by water and earth.

Next, you will cense the object. (*Cense* means to waft incense smoke over the object.)

With the incense smoke, cense and say:
I bless and charge you with air and fire.

Cense and asperge the string/yarn and say:
I cleanse and consecrate you by water and earth.
I bless and charge you with air and fire.

Hold the red string/yarn in your hands and say:
Tiny bundle of String/yarn, you are now the same as the bonds between me and "Name of person."

Tie one end of the string/yarn to the object and then encircle your waist with the other end of the string/yarn, while you say:
You are the bonds that connect us now.
From me to "Name of person" and from "Name of person" to me.
Our connection is by thee.

Sit and concentrate on the bond between you both and see it as the string/yarn that now connects you and the object. Once you have a firm connection with that thought, take the boline and cut the string/yarn, seeing in your mind's eye the astral bonds are being cut along with the string/yarn.

Once you complete the cut, say:
I am now free of the ties of "Name of person" as he/she is of me.
May my happiness expand, and may "Name of person's" happiness expand.
Blessed be.

Finish up with the cakes and wine part of the ritual and then close the circle.

And you're done.

Separating ourselves from toxic people is important for our happiness and well-being. It even blesses the life of the other person. You are doing yourself and the other person a favor.

I trust that this ritual will help you be happier and healthier.

Section Five
Protect Yourself #7

Simple House Protection Ritual

Over the years, sometimes, I hear of someone who wants to protect their house from intrusion. Here is a Simple House Protection Ritual.

What you will need:
- Picture of your house and family
- Pentacle
- 5 Chime candles, one of each: Red, Blue, Yellow, White, Green
- Protection oil to dress the candles
- Loadstone (or a magnet)
- Lighter
- Pen, magickal ink and virgin paper

Preparation:
Place candles, oil, loadstone and pentagram on the altar.

Cast the Circle.

Cleanse and Consecrate your items (candles, loadstone, pentacle, and picture). Dress all candles and the loadstone.

Place colored candles in their appropriate points on the pentagram. (see picture below)

Place your picture of home and family on the pentagram.
Red-Fire
Yellow-Air
Blue-Water
Green-Earth
White-Spirit

Use the pen and write the following on the sheet of paper. Start with the letter "c." Write the below charm.

```
        c
       ect
      tect
     otecti
    rotectio
   Protection
```

Place the protection paper charm onto the pentacle on top of the picture of your home and family.

Rub the loadstone on the charm and say:
 Clickity clackity nip nap knakaty,
Save me now from society's insanity.
Round, round my home, flies protection's lovely cone
Protecting me now from our society's sick own.
Circling around my precious ones and home,
Secure and safe now we can weather any storm.

So Mote It Be.

Place the loadstone on top of the charm and photo.
Take your lighter and light the first of the five candles (Red-Fire) and say:

As my spirit burns with desire, this spell has begun. I burn all hate and ill will from harming this, my home, and the loved ones within.

Light the second of the five candles (Yellow-Air) and say:

With my breath, I breathe life into this spell that all hate and ill will be blown away from this, my home, and the loved ones within.

Light the third of the five candles (Blue-Water) and say:

With the salty tides of life and birth, I wash away all hate and ill will away from this, my home, and the loved ones within.

Light the fourth of the five candles (Green-Earth) and say:

I ground this spell into reality that all hate and ill will be grounded peacefully away from this, my home, and the loved ones within.

Light the fifth of the five candles (White-Spirit) and say:

As above so below, safety is mine for all in my home to hold.

Sit and meditate and see a sphere of energy surround your home.

Do the Cakes and Wine Ceremony.

Close the Circle.

* * *

May this ritual serve you well.

Section Five
Protect Yourself #8

The Wiccan Badass Protects Herself from Toxic People

Many of us deal with toxic people in our lives. As I write this section, I have just seen a truly toxic presidential election (of 2016). It was a surprise to a number people that one of the biggest bullies (who had been caught doing numerous terrible things) has been elected President of the USA.

This brings my thoughts to: *How do we deal with bullies and toxic people?* I'll share four methods here:

1. Get away from toxic people

If you assess that someone is toxic, decide to protect yourself and get away from that person.

Keep away from people who drain your energy both physically and psychologically.

Make good choices. Limit your exposure to toxic people. I'm including the decision to limit your exposure to toxic people whether on social media or TV.

Some of us have family members who are toxic. In that case, limit your exposure when possible.

Stay aware of your own personal energy. Make the tough decisions—that's what a Wiccan Badass does.

2. Stand up for yourself

Don't let a toxic person step all over you. Fight for yourself.

How do you do that? First, you can begin by using assertive words.

I heard of a person who stood up for herself. She said, "I'm here to work, not to listen to racist jokes. I'm here in this office. You can keep such jokes for your buddies at the loading dock."

In many cases, you are the only one who will stand up for you. It does take practice. You might even want to rehearse with a friend so you know what to say in a particular situation.

When abuse occurs, don't just roll over and take it. Be assertive and stand up for yourself and others.

Remember, Wiccans are *not* pacifists!

When you're standing up for yourself, you will get resistance. My friend Dina told her boyfriend, "That's it. You hit me on the arm once. You're going to therapy now. Or we're through. And if you hit me again. I'm gone. Understand?"

Dina understood that if something is wrong, ignoring it can do *more* harm.

Stop the offending person from doing more harm. Speak up. Tell the person what *you* will do.

3. Keep yourself safe

On the physical level, you can remove yourself from dangerous situations. Additionally, you can choose to avoid placing yourself in dangerous situations in the first place. One martial arts master says, "The best defense is *not* to be there."

On the spiritual level, you can use the process known as "shielding" (that I mentioned earlier). Shielding keeps a toxic person from feeding off your energy. It also helps protect you from any negative energy they toss at you.

How to Do Shielding:

Go to someplace safe. You could even do your brief shielding process in a bathroom stall. Breathe in and out—and feel your feet on the ground. Reach down with your consciousness and take a deep breath. Visualize pulling up the energy of Mother Earth through your feet and up your body.

Continue to pull the energy into your chest, then up to the top of your head. Then with your arms, push the energy out into a sphere around you. Envision a white, greenish light surrounding you. Concentrate for a moment to make sure the sphere of light is stable. Know that no bad energies can reach you with your shield up. Feel the strength of the shield. *You are now shielded.*

In some situations, you may have to call for support, perhaps, a family member of even support from the police.

Do what's necessary. Keep yourself safe.

4. Declare toxic-free zones

Consciously choose to relax and focus on that which is positive. Declare a toxic-free zone, that is, tell friends and family not to mention the toxic person during dinner time, for example.

Additionally, you can go to a place of peace and tranquility such as a temple room. Take a walk in a park.

Many Wiccans find that meditation is a way for them to create a toxic-free time for relaxation and renewal.

Section Five
Protect Yourself #9

How to Remove Black Magic from One's Home

To remove bad energies from your home you can do a house blessing.

House Blessing
What you will need:
- Large container of Kosher Sea Salt
- One white candle
- Spring or purified water (enough to asperge your entire home)
- Bowl (small)
- Bowl (large)
- Pitcher (this holds water for refilling your large bowl)
- Incense
- Anointing oil
- Athame

- White altar cloth
- Pentacle
- Bell

Set up your altar with the white candle (representing Fire) and the other Three Elements (Air, Water, and Earth). Put the white candle in the middle and the other Elements on their sides of the altar. Pour some water into the large bowl. Set the small bowl on the West side.

Section off the house with salt by making boundary lines blocking entryways for each room with the salt. (Set the salt in lines.) This will contain the energy in each room so that you can work on it as an individual space.

Start with blessing and purifying each Element by placing your athame in each Element–and say:

For the white candle: Light the candle, then place athame over it and say:

I consecrate and bless this flame in the names of the Great Lord of the Sun and Gracious Lady of the Moon, that this flame be Their sacred light to cast out all darkness with its use.

Water Blessing:

I consecrate and bless this water in the names of the Great Lord of the Sun and Gracious Lady of the Moon, that this water be Their fertile energy to create new blessings with its use.

Salt Blessing:

I consecrate and bless this salt in the names of the Great Lord of the Sun and Gracious Lady of the Moon, that this salt be Their loving bodies to grow new hope with its use.

Incense Blessing:
I consecrate and bless this incense in the names of the Great Lord of the Sun and Gracious Lady of the Moon, that this incense be Their sacred breath to breathe new and positive stories with its use.

Take three pinches of salt and mix with the Blessed Water. Place incense on charcoal—or if using stick incense, light the incense-stick using the white candle.
Bless the oil with the Elements saying:
I purify you with earth and water.
I cleanse with fire and air.

Dip the small bowl into the large bowl to scoop up some Blessed Water.
Move around the space first with the water, asperge and say while going in deocil (clockwise):
I purify you with earth and water.
Ring the Bell.

Next, move around the space while fanning the smoke of the burning incense and say:
I cleanse you with fire and air.
Ring the Bell.

If you sense any more negative energy, guide it with your hands. Direct the negative energy to the large bowl of holy water so that it is absorbed and cleansed. Shake the energy off your hands as you place your hands over the water bowl.
After purifying and cleansing the space, take up the athame and go to an entryway and trace a banishing pentagram there and say:
I cast out all baneful energies and seal this [Door or

Window or Fireplace]

Then take up the oil and dab on each corner of the door frame/window/fireplace saying:

You are now closed to all negative and baneful energies.

Once done, move to next room, and start all over again.

When you have completed the ritual for the whole house, pour the last batch of the holy water down a sewage drain that goes away from the house.

This will help you clear all the nasties and bad energy from your home. You can also smudge your home afterwards just to make sure.

You deserve to enjoy your home in peace and harmony.

Section Five
Protect Yourself #10

How A Wiccan Can Relieve Worries

When it comes to self-protection, sometimes we need to protect our peace of mind. As a Wiccan, I have had many worries over the years, and I have found this chant to be helpful.

The Gods' Presence Chant
Though the darkness presses in,
I know the Gods' presence within.
Open the Door for my Insights' flight,
May this be solved in a fortnight.

Section Six
Know You're Here to Serve

My mentor, as the High Priestess, lit a candle, which began our *Rite for the Departed.*

I could feel my heart start to unwind. I had taken it really hard that my friend, Joe, had passed away. He had committed suicide, and I still recalled the last time I saw him alive.

He had driven three hours from a faraway city.

I asked, "Would you like to get a cup of coffee or see a movie?"

He said, "Not really. I'm fine right here."

He sat in the central chair in our living room. He was in such good spirits. He looked content. I know he enjoyed his visits because there is love and warmth in my home with my sweetheart.

But now Joe was gone.

I can still hear his laughter. Joe had this comical way of putting his hands over his ears and saying, "Too much information! Too much information!"

Now, during the Rite of the Departed, my mentor, acting as the High Priestess, was serving our coven and helping all of us gathered to shift our energy around the grief over deaths of departed friends.

The Wiccan Badass has a special form of knowledge. She knows that she is here to serve.

When you serve, that is, help others, you tap into Real Power. God and Goddess guide us. Such guidance strengthens each of us on our individual path. Still, there is a united path that we walk in our community.

As you serve others, you are immersed in a pool of energy. The process strengthens them; it strengthens you.

As I mentioned earlier, my definition of a Wiccan Badass is someone who does these three things:
- Seizes choices
- Gains knowledge
- Acts decisively

In Section Six, we will discuss a number of details about appropriately contributing to the lives of others.

Just recently, my sweetheart and I felt distraught when we heard that his 86-year-old mother fell near her home in a city quite distant from where we live. His mother's injuries required surgery.

We found some peace when we went into action to help her. My sweetheart also brightened up when he did some volunteer work to help others.

I'll put this bluntly: The Wiccan Badass is full of positive and powerful energy more often. Learning to appropriately serve others is a great source of renewal and new positive energy.

We are meant to be in the flow of life and to engage in

making a contribution to others.

You're here to help other people and the environment. In a way, you even help God and Goddess when you take good care of Their creations.

You can express your personal power by volunteering. Perhaps, you're called to help at a soup kitchen.

I've personally volunteered at the Peninsula Humane Society.

Our next section is about conducting a ritual to help another person.

Section Six
Know You're Here to Serve #1

What to Do When Conducting Ritual for Another Person

Below I'm including a ritual that I was invited to create to help a friend to sell her house. This ties into our focus on "know you're here to serve."

Here are three vital components to conducting a ritual for another person:
1) Secure their permission.
2) Ask them what they need.
3) Customize your language (in the spell or ritual) to what they need.
4) Work with them so they are comfortable in participating in the ritual.

Note that the person's energy is a vital component of making the spell or ritual yield a great outcome.

Using a Ritual to Help You Sell a House (or something else)

"There's no other solution," my friend said. "I need to sell my house. Can you help me to sell it for a great price? I want the funds for schooling and even to help with my retirement." She asked for a ritual for such a purpose.

This ritual is written for two people: One to beat the drum and one to perform the actions. One person can do this ritual by simply using recorded music.

Ritual for Selling a House

What you will need:
- 8 white tea lights
- 8 slips of paper with a desire and need from the house (to put under the 8 white tea light candles)
- Basket for tea lights
- 4 tea lights for the quarter candles
- Picture of House
- 1 Green candle (Chime candle preferred)
- Drum
- Lighter or matches
- Candle Holder
- Money Oil
- Candle Snuffer
- A short poem of thanks and blessings.
- Taper to light candles
- Cakes and Wine

Warning: Ritual should be done on a waxing moon.

Set up:
Set up places for the tea light candles to be placed in a circle—equally-spaced around the altar. (You'll place the candles in their spots later). Set up the altar in the middle of the circle with a picture of the house to be sold, money oil and green candle on the pentacle. Fill the basket with the eight tea light candles. Place the basket on the altar.

Cast Circle as usual.

Have a priest or priestess start a slow drum beat.

Owner (the House Owner) takes the basket of tea lights and lights the first tea light (of eight), using the working candle. Owner places the lit tea light candle into the first position (at the North point)—of the eight tea light candle positions. Owner says:

My friend, you were there sheltering me in the cold of December, I am grateful for you.

The slow drum beat continues.

Owner takes the second tea light out of the basket and lights it from the first tea light (already lit). Owner places the second tea light to the right (at the North-East point) of the first tea light, and says:

My friend, you were there when the first whispers of Spring were in the air, I am grateful for you.

Owner takes the third tea light out of the basket and lights it from the second tea light (already lit). Owner places the third tea light to the right (at the East point) of the second tea light, and says:

My friend, you were there for me when the Spring Showers washed the last of the cold winter away, I am grateful for you.

Owner takes the fourth tea light out of the basket and lights it from the third tea light (already lit). Owner places the fourth tea light to the right (at the East/South point) of the third tea light, and says:

My friend, you were married to my heart and were the center of my world, I am grateful for you.

Owner takes the fifth tea light out of the basket and lights it from the fourth tea light (already lit). Owner places the fifth tea light to the right (at the South point) of the fourth tea light, and says:

My friend, you were here when I needed you to shelter me from the heat of Summer, I am grateful for you.

Owner takes the sixth tea light out of the basket and lights it from the fifth tea light (already lit). Owner places the sixth tea light to the right (at the South/West point) of the fifth tea light, and says:

My friend, you were there helping me have stability so I could harvest the first fruits of my labors, I am grateful for you.

Owner takes the seventh tea light out of the basket and lights it from the sixth tea light. Owner places the seventh tea light to the right (at the West point) of the sixth tea light, and says:

My friend, you are here for me in my time of need. I am grateful for you.

Owner takes the eighth tea light out of the basket and lights it from the seventh tea light. Owner places the eighth tea light to the right (at the North/West point) of the seventh tea light, and says:

My friend, thank you for the support you have given me, I am grateful for you.

Owner takes the now empty basket to the first position of North (and the first candle) and bows to the first candle.
Owner places the basket near the altar.
Drum beat stops.
Owner picks up the picture of her home and says:
(Owner recites her short poem of thanks and blessings for the house and states what she needs it to do for her now.)

Owner then places the picture on the pentacle and begins dressing the green candle while saying:

Rub, rub, rub, with money oil I do,
Singing my deepest desires to you.

Little green candle bring me wealth,
Help me sell my house by the twelfth.
Money comes in and my debt goes away,
Helping me finance my future today.

So mote it be.

Owner places the green candle into its holder and holds it up and concentrates on her desire. She then lights the green candle with the working candle. She places the green candle (in its holder) on top of the picture of her home and recites the poem.

A priest or priestess starts beating the drum again.

Owner picks up the snuffer and takes it to the Eighth (the West/North point) of the eight tea light candle positions says:

I need now from you __(reads from first slip of paper)__

Then Owner snuffs out the tea light candle and then bows.

Owner picks up the snuffer and takes it to the Seventh (the West point) of the eight tea light candle positions says:

I need now from you __(reads from second slip of paper)__

Then Owner snuffs out the tea light candle and then bows.

Owner picks up the snuffer and takes it to the Sixth (the West/South point) of the eight tea light candle positions says:

I need now from you __(reads from third slip of paper)__

Then Owner snuffs out the tea light candle and then bows.

Owner picks up the snuffer and takes it to the Fifth (the South point) of the eight tea light candle positions says:

I need now from you __(reads from fourth slip of paper)__

Then Owner snuffs out the tea light candle and then bows.

Owner picks up the snuffer and takes it to the Fourth (the South/East point) of the eight tea light candle positions says:

I need now from you __(reads from fifth slip of paper)__

Then Owner snuffs out the tea light candle and then bows.

Owner picks up the snuffer and takes it to the Third (the East point) of the eight tea light candle positions says:

I need now from you __(reads from sixth slip of paper)__

Then Owner snuffs out the tea light candle and then bows.

Owner picks up the snuffer and takes it to the Second (the North/East point) of the eight tea light candle positions says:

I need now from you __(reads from seventh slip of paper)__

Then Owner snuffs out the tea light candle and then bows.

Owner picks up the snuffer and takes it to the First (the North point) of the eight tea light candle positions says:

I need now from you __(reads from eighth slip of paper)__

Then Owner snuffs out the tea light candle and then bows.

Drum beat stops.
Do the Cakes and Wine Ceremony.
Close the Circle.

Section Six
Know You're Here to Serve #2

Know the Difference between "Helping" and "Serving"

Some time ago, I tried to help my sweetheart to begin a consistent meditation practice. Lord and Lady knows that he certainly needs something to calm him down! He does a lot, at a fast pace, with his work. He's an entrepreneur, and work fills his thoughts.

So, I led him through a couple of guided meditations. Still, he just didn't make time to put meditation into his life.

The problem was I was trying to help him, but I was not helping him the way that he needed to be served.

The point here is **"helping" is when we use what we know and what we're used to.**

Instead, *serving* **is about asking the person about what he or she needs.**

So how did things work out with my sweetheart? He found some research that emphasizes that when we concentrate on viewing one object and listen to one sound simultaneously, then our brain "goes into neutral."

So, for over two months, every morning, my sweetheart stares at a candle while making the "ahhhhh" sound for three minutes. It works for him.

You might say that **serving is a sacred thing** and "helping" is an ego thing.

We fall back on helping because that's what we're used to. It's also the easier action.

The question is: "How do you know what would be 'serving'?"

This would be a good opportunity to meditate and ask for guidance from God and Goddess.

Additionally, ask the person about what he or she really needs.

So, if you were going to do a ritual for someone, first get their permission. Then, ask, "What are you hoping to get out of this?" and "What do you really need?"

See if you need to quiet down your automatic response of "trying to be helpful."

Remember that each person is on his or her own sacred path. Just because you have trodden on a particular trail, it does not mean that this path serves them.

Make sure you ask what they really need and truly serve them.

Section Six
Know You're Here to Serve #3

Know Your Part and Know When to Let Go

As a Wiccan Badass, you can do your part, but a Wiccan Badass knows when to step aside.

Sometimes, people come us and say they need help. Upon reflection, we may come to realize that a specific person must hit bottom or go through a rough patch. There are times when you just have to let go and let the person walk their own path—in their own timing.

Sometimes, readers have contacted me and said that they had several people conduct spells on their behalf.

For example, one person, "Alex," said that he had spells done on his behalf for a specific problem, but nothing got better.

After a conversation, I realized that some details indicated that Alex was blocking change.

In the moment, I felt the intuition to ask, "Could it be that you're blocking something here? Sometimes, we block change because we're getting something out of the status quo. I hear you: You sound miserable. I'm just wondering if there is something that you're getting in the current situation."

I said this gently. Still, Alex came back with lots of energy and big denials. Sometimes, that's a sign that the person is stuck. Especially, when the person simply refuses to consider what you've said.

This section is about "Know Your Part and Know When to Let Go."

Perhaps, you've seen this. You want to help someone but *that person needs to do the work herself.*

You can do something to be supportive. Maybe, listen well during a conversation.

And, at some point, you need to have your own boundaries.

Boundaries are very important for the Wiccan Badass. Making and keeping your boundaries is key to a healthy and safe life. Just as we put up our energy shields, we need to have verbal boundaries, too. If you don't, you're just going to get walked all over by people and even noncorporal entities. So how do we put up our boundaries?

Identifying Your Boundaries
Take a piece of paper and write down different situations or one situation at hand. What are you *not* willing to accept regarding this situation?

Next to each situation, note what you really think is unacceptable to you.

You might write something like: *I will not be yelled at. If someone persists, I will leave the room.*

Now read your boundaries aloud.

When you can, practice stating your boundaries with a supportive friend.

You may find that it is hard to say your boundaries aloud. Still, stay with this practice. It's important to state your boundaries aloud.

To stand firm on your new decision, you need to free yourself from conditioning from the past. When we're under pressure we tend to fall back into our old settings. So, to override your old habits, you'll need to keep with your practice of stating your boundaries aloud.

Developing and protecting your boundaries is a deep topic. There are whole books dedicated to this process.

Here I want to emphasize that **strong boundaries make a strong witch.**

In the meantime, here is a chant to help you stay firm on your boundaries:

Boundaries, boundaries all around,
Keep them up so they don't come down.
Firmly placed like brick and mortar,
Shall not chip, and will give no quarter.
God and Goddess I know you care.
Keep me strong, that's my prayer.

Your Wiccan Badass Path Continues

As we complete this journey with this book, I celebrate your efforts and spiritual growth.

Please continue your path with me by viewing my articles at my blog at GoddessHasYourBack.com

Let's look at how far we have come. We began with my thoughts on being a badass, *someone who makes her own choices.* Someone who has more great moments in life because she or he takes action. This person has more capacity to handle tough things that arise in life.

A Wiccan Badass tunes into the power and love from God and Goddess.

We discussed the **Six Actions of being a Wiccan Badass:**

1. Connect with God and Goddess.
2. Be smart and knowledgeable.
3. Have energy.
4. Make things happen.
5. Protect yourself.
6. Know you're here to serve.

Additionally, I included my thoughts on how **a Wiccan Badass is someone who does these three things:**
- Seizes choices
- Gains knowledge
- Acts decisively

From this point forward, consider learning more about rituals, chants, tips, and ways to customize your rituals just for you ... and even more material when you sign up for my exclusive enewsletters. Just go to GoddessHasYourBack.com and click on the link (on the right side of the webpage).

Consider my previous five books. Thank you.

Blessed Be,
Moonwater SilverClaw

ABOUT THE AUTHOR

Moonwater SilverClaw is a Wiccan High Priestess and member of the Covenant of the Goddess and the New Wiccan Church. She has trained people new to Wicca. Her personal story reveals how Wicca saved her life and helped her strengthen herself to secure her release from an abusive marriage.

Moonwater has been practicing Wicca since 1990, first as a solitary and then in a coven.

Moonwater posts at her blog,

GoddessHasYourBack.com

[with visitors from 173 countries]

She felt called to write the blog and write 6 books even though she is dyslexic. She works with a team of editors. She says, "I wish to educate those who don't understand what the Craft is about. Some people may not yet identify themselves as Pagan, but they'd like more information."

Moonwater has addressed college students in Comparative Religion classes for over ten years. She leads workshops. She lives with her cat Magick and her sweetheart of many years; he is one of her editors. She enjoys knitting and photography.

Her work is endorsed by Wiccan notables including Patrick McCollum (receiver of the Mahatma Gandhi Award for the Advancement of Religious Pluralism).

Moonwater SilverClaw can be contacted at:
AskAWitchNow@gmail.com
Or at her blog:
GoddessHasYourBack.com

Special Offer Just for Readers of this Book:

Contact Moonwater SilverClaw at askawitchnow@gmail.com for special discounts on books, consulting, workshops and presentations. Just mention your experience with this book.

Excerpt from
Goddess Has Your Back

by Moonwater SilverClaw

CHAPTER 1:
GODDESS HAS YOUR BACK

Would you like your Wiccan path to lift up your self-esteem?

Would you simply like to feel better?

This book helps you actually feel your connection with the Goddess on a daily basis—even moment to moment.

As I mentioned in my first two books, *The Hidden Children of the Goddess* and *Beyond the Law of Attraction to Real Magick*, Wicca saved my life and empowered me to leave an abusive marriage.

As a High Priestess, I have supported friends, family, and colleagues in times of need. My blog TheHiddenChildrenoftheGoddess.com gives me a weekly opportunity to support website visitors from over 173 countries.

This book gives *us* the space and time to really explore magickal practices, rituals, meditations and experiences that you'll find comforting and uplifting.

My journey upon this path began with meeting the Gods. The Gods showed me the true path to self love and acceptance. Where I saw nothingness and unworthiness, they showed me abundance and a unique specialness that I had.

Now I will let you in on a secret. *You have your own unique specialness that no one else has.* It is yours, and yours alone.

This new path is yours to discover and walk. Just like my own path, your path is a beautiful discovery simply waiting for you. Prepare to step forward on this new, wondrous, and beautiful path.

Let's take the next step.

Secret of How to Do Magick

When I first started doing magick it was really hit or miss, most often *mess*. My spell work was just not as effective as I wanted it to be. What was I doing wrong?

If you have wondered the same thing, you have probably done similar mistakes. For example, I'd do a money spell, but I'd just get new problems!

The real problem was, like many people, I just wanted a big payday. What I didn't know was that this is really the wrong way to approach a lack of money.

Many, if not most, spells written today are focused on the external opportunities or even requesting gifts from the Gods. Focusing on just the external can create new problems.

What if I could tell you a **Secret of how to do magick**—in a way where you avoid ethics issues about money?

I have mentored a number of people about this *Secret*. Now I will share with you this Secret.

A phrase from the poem by Doreen Valiente entitled *The Charge of the Goddess* tells us how to do magick well. But many of us, like my younger self, just don't see it. The line I'm talking about is: "…if that which thou seekest thou findest not within thee, thou wilt never find it without thee."

This line invites us to look within as we approach our magickal work.

Instead of focusing on how to get money from outside sources, focus within. How? Instead of asking for a handout from the universe, ask, **"How I can create more energy in** myself to obtain my desire? How can I make myself open to more prosperity?"

Let's get more specific. You have been laid off and need a new job pronto! Bills are pilling up fast.

Let's use a sigil for this purpose.

How to Make Your Own Personal Sigils

Imagine putting a magical intention into an object. Why would you do that? Wiccans do this because they want the object to hold power to help them realize a personal desire. For example, you may be job hunting and you want the power of the object—in this case, a sigil—to assist you to get the ideal job.

Making your own personal sigils is easy. Some time ago, author/artist Austin Osman Spare devised a method for creating sigils.

Since that time, a number of authors have discussed Austin Osman Spare's process of making sigils. One book I appreciate is Frater U. D.'s *Practical Sigil Magic: Creating Personal Symbols for Success.*

I have made a couple of my own additions to the process.

First, throughout history, witches made sigils out of virgin parchment. But that is quite expensive. Also, if you're vegan and will not wear leather, you will want to use something else. Why? Parchment is typically made from sheep skin. So, let's talk about a process devoid of parchment.

I use the heavier art paper, the kind that absorbs ink and which can be infused with different tinctures made with herbs. Watercolor paper is a nice choice, too.

What about inks? You could use one of the many magickal inks on the market. My favorite is Dragons Blood Ink. But magickal inks can be expensive. So, you can make your own out of a high-grade ink such as Winsor Newton ink or India ink. To make it a magickal ink just add some essential oil to it, like myrrh. Mix and consecrate.

You can even use Sharpie pens as author Peter Paddon suggests. Just make sure to designate specific pens for only magickal work. They'll be part of your set of magickal tools.

You can use different colors for different desires. Here is a short list of colors and meanings that I include in my book *The Hidden Children of the Goddess:*

- Red: sex, desire, vitality, strength
- Orange: charm, confidence, joy, persuasion
- Yellow: intellectual development, joy, intellectual strength
- Green: prosperity, abundance, fertility, money matters
- Blue: healing, protection, spiritual development
- Purple: the occult, power, magick
- Pink: love, friendship, compassion
- White: purity, innocence, peace, tranquility

Write out your desire on a scratch piece of paper; you can use a single word or a phrase. Some examples are:

- I want an ideal job for me at this time
- Happiness
- I need a new house
- Success

We'll now use the word "Success" as our example. Cross off all the repeat letters in Success. You end up with S, U, C, and E. (You want only one of each letter that appears in the word.) Next, scramble the letters, getting S, E, U, and C (for example).

Now comes the fun part: Combine the letters together in

an image.

Success Sigil

Can you find the letters?

In this way, you can make all sorts of sigils.

If you want to imbue it with a potion or tincture, this is the time to do it. You can either soak the paper in your tincture or brush it on. Either way you must let it dry. Overnight is best.

Now with this new image (of combined letters), inscribe it with your magical ink on your absorbent paper.

Now that you have the sigil, the next step is to breathe life into it with Pranic Breathing, also known as belly breathing. If you're familiar with yoga, you are probably familiar with Pranic Breathing techniques. Breathe in deeply; allow your stomach to inflate. Visualize pulling up energy from the earth. When you have built up enough energy in your lungs, blow it onto the sigil. This will charge it with your energy and further empower your intention.

Now place your sigil in a safe place and forget about it. Forgetting about it is the toughest part of the whole process. This helps the magick work.

As you can see, making your own sigils is quite easy and fun. After some practice, you will be able to do them quickly and easily.

Remember the Gods are here to help. You can call on them for inner strength.

How to phrase a sentence for a sigil to get a job:
- All blocks I have put up, known and unknown, dissolve so that I am a good candidate and my future employer hires me.
- Help me express the inner strength, skills and energy so that I can acquire a job of my liking.

Here are phrases for those who have an interest in an entrepreneurial path:
- I find new ways to serve others successfully so that money comes to me naturally.
- All blocks I have put up, known and unknown, dissolve so that I can create abundance in my life.

Can you see how each sentence or phrase focuses on inner change, not the external "give me, give me"? With these phrases, you are not looking for a handout. **You are creating the abundance by changing *yourself*.**

This can be applied to the rest of your magick as well. Another example is love spells. Focus your magick on *being more loving, or more open to love*. Never do love spells *upon* a particular person. Instead do a spell to attract love to you in whatever form is appropriate by creating yourself as more loving.

By focusing on inner change and developing our inner strengths, we can achieve our desires.

Goddess Has Your Back in the Worst Times

When you're reading a book, what are you looking for? I'm looking for the truth and some way to become stronger. I promise to provide both for you in this chapter.

END OF EXCERPT
from *Goddess Has Your Back*
Available from top online retailers

* * * * * *

Beyond the Law of Attraction to Real Magick
How You Can Remove Blocks to Prosperity, Happiness and Inner Peace (Excerpt by Moonwater SilverClaw)

Self-perspective: Overcome the Blockage of Not Feeling Worthy

Do you feel worthy of the best that life has to offer? Maybe on the conscious level you say, "Sure. Bring it on. The new house, new car, and a real, loving relationship."

But have you ever sabotaged your chances of getting exactly what you wanted?

Self-sabotage can occur because of feeling not worthy on a subconscious level.

If it's subconscious, how can we deal with this?

Good question.

Soon I will share with you a Self-Love Meditation.

But first let's talk about magick. The whole premise of this book is that there is a way to go about the Law of Attraction with more power.

To put it simply, the Law of Attraction is a form of magick, but people who read an introductory book on the

Law of Attraction are often denied enough information to truly make the Law of Attraction work in their own lives.

So, to really make a positive difference in your life, we need to talk about real magick. I spell magick with a "k" to distinguish it from stage magic you see on television.

Magick is a natural power, *not* a supernatural one. Who uses magick? In my spiritual path, Wicca, one is trained to use magick in appropriate ways.

When Wiccans do magick, they channel *natural* energies and create change with them.

Well, if Wicca isn't really supernatural then why practice Wicca at all?

To put it simply, *you want something.* That's probably why you were interested in the Law of Attraction in the first place. Now in the context of learning real magick, you'll be able to fully use the Law of Attraction. And that's good news!

Everyone is different and has their own answer to that question. I like to think of religion as a bottle of wine. Let's say you have three different people who all taste the same bottle of wine. The first person points out that the flavor has accents of oak. The second praises the hints of apple in it, and the third enjoys the floral notes. They are all right. The wine contains all the flavors they described. But each person detected something different. Religion is like that. Deity can't be entirely known. So, the truth of it is scattered into many faiths.

In Wicca, we honor the God and the Goddess. If that's new to you, you can substitute the label of Higher Power or God or Deity.

The Gods and Goddesses have helped me and they can help you, too. The first thing they taught me was self-love.

Before we go further, let's make a distinction between

self-love and self-conceit (or being stuck in one's ego).

Self-love is about kindness and support. So, it's a good thing. It is NOT about your ego or puffing yourself up.

Let me show you how the Gods changed my perspective on myself for the better.

One of the best exercises I learned is meditation. Through reflective meditation, the Gods helped me understand how skewed my perception of myself really was. This was a key turning point for me.

One thing you always hear about are affirmations, but for many of us these just don't work.

First, let's cover what an affirmation is. It's a personal, positive statement. It can be as simple as "I feel terrific" or "I make a lot of money."

For many, the above statements don't work. Why?

A number of people have said, "It just sounds like I'm lying to myself."

Like myself, many people's inner self-beliefs interfere with these positive statements. For an example, if I used the affirmation "I am thin," my brain would object with "No, I'm not. Look in the mirror." It's not true. No matter how hard you try to pound that new idea into your brain, your brain pounds just as hard back.

So how did the Gods help me deal with this problem? They inspired me to create a Self-Love Meditation.

So instead of the uphill battle of an affirmation, we'll use the Self-Love Meditation to work with the situation.

END OF EXCERPT from *Beyond the Law of Attraction to Real Magick*

Purchase your copy of the above books (paperback or ebook) at top online retailers.

See **Free Chapters** of Moonwater SilverClaw's 6 books at a top online retailer.

www.ingramcontent.com/pod-product-compliance
Lightning Source LLC
Chambersburg PA
CBHW060536100426
42743CB00009B/1548